Elements of Fortification

ELEMENTS

OF

FORTIFICATION.

ELEMENTS

OF

FORTIFICATION:

FIELD AND PERMANENT.

FOR

THE USE OF STUDENTS, CIVILIAN AND MILITARY.

BY

CAPTAIN A. F. LENDY,

DIRECTOR OF THE PRACTICAL MILITARY COLLEGE OF SUNBURY,
LATE OF THE FRENCH STAFF, ETC. ETC.

LONDON:
JOHN W. PARKER AND SON, WEST STRAND.
1857.

TO HIS ROYAL HIGHNESS

THE DUKE OF CAMBRIDGE, K.G.

ETC. ETC.

COMMANDING-IN-CHIEF HER MAJESTY'S FORCES,

THIS WORK

IS,

BY HIS ROYAL HIGHNESS'S GRACIOUS PERMISSION,

MOST RESPECTFULLY

DEDICATED,

BY HIS OBEDIENT HUMBLE SERVANT,

A. F. LENDY.

PREFACE.

FORTIFICATION has long been considered the exclusive province of the Engineer; it has been hidden from profane eyes by a thick cloud of technicalities and minutiæ of plan drawing, geometry, &c. Hence the small number of Officers of the Line familiar with its elements.

In the following pages I have endeavoured to bring these elements within the reach of every one, by carefully avoiding all puzzling and needless detail, and confining myself to the *spirit* and *substance* of the science.

Those of my readers who are already acquainted with the most elementary principles of geometry will be able to construct on paper a front of Vauban, or any other work, with all the accuracy required for the examination for Her Majesty's Service.

Those who do not possess these principles will nevertheless, I trust, understand the science, and become sufficiently familiar with it for all Field purposes. To these in particular I address myself; and to encourage them, and show them that they may still become good Engineers, I have only to point out Maréchal Comte de Pagan, a most distinguished military engineer, who knew nothing of drawing, projections, &c., and did not begin his studies until after he had lost his sight.

Both classes of readers must, however, bear in mind that it is not by reading a single book that they can become masters of the science; but that it is by perusing the records of campaigns, and availing themselves of the experience they contain.

The limits of this elementary treatise do not allow me to enter into great historical details; I have, therefore, merely indicated the chief sources whence further information may be derived, whenever opportunity offers.

A. F. LENDY.

Sunbury, May, 1857.

TABLE OF CONTENTS.

___

CHAPTER I.

PAGE

DEFINITIONS. 13

Sec. I. ON FIRING 14
   Direct, Oblique, and Enfilade Fire 15
   Slanting, Reverse, Cross, Flank, and Vertical Fire . . . 16
   Ricochet, Pitching, and Plunging Fire 17

Sec. II. DITCH AND COVERING MASS 17
   Parapet, Slopes, Banquette 20
   Rampart, Relief, Command 21
   Escarp, Counterscarp, Berm 22
   Depth, Width 23
   Glacis, Covered Way 24

Sec. III. OUTLINE 25
   Salient and Re-entering Angles 25
   Intrenchment, Epaulment, Outline 26
   Line of Fire, Master-line 26
   Profiles, Right, Oblique, Extreme 26

Sec. IV. PROPERTIES OF THE OUTLINE. 28
   Undefended Angle 29
   Dead Angle 30
   Limits of their Opening 30
   Dimensions of Faces 31
   Fundamental Principles 33

CHAPTER II.

PAGE

Sec. I. NOMENCLATURE OF FIELD WORKS 35
Isolated Works and Lines 35
Open Works 35
Enclosed Works 38
Blockhouses 40
Lines 42
Bastions 46

Sec. II. SELECTION OF AN OUTLINE 49
Influence of the Ground 49
Strength of a Garrison 52
Dimensions of Enclosed Works 52
Maxima and Minima of Field-Works 53

CHAPTER III.

DEFENCE OF FIELD-WORKS 56

Sec. I. ARTILLERY 56
Barbette, Embrasure 57

Sec. II. a. DEFENCE OF THE DITCH 59
Stockade, Caponier, Gallery of Counterscarp 60
Retirade 62

Sec. II. b. OBSTACLES 62
Palisades 63
Fraises, Stockades 64
Tambours, Abattis 65
Chevaux-de-Frise 66
Pickets, Crows' Feet 67
Military Pits, Fougasses 68
Inundations 70

Sec. III. DEFENCE AND ATTACK OF FIELD-WORKS . . . 71
Interior Intrenchments 73

CHAPTER IV.

PAGE

CONSTRUCTION OF WORKS 76
Profiling 76
Excavation 77
Revetments 79
Sods, Fascines, Gabions 80
Hurdles, Sandbags, Planks 81
Communications 82
Bridges 84
Defilading 84

CHAPTER V.

Sec. I. PERMANENT FORTIFICATION 90
Rampart, Bulwark 92
Bastion, Polygon, Front 93
Regular and Irregular Fortification 94
Systems 94
Sec. II. VAUBAN'S FIRST SYSTEM 95
Plan 96
Profiles 100

CHAPTER VI.

ATTACK AND DEFENCE OF A FORTRESS 108

Sec. I. IRREGULAR ATTACKS 108
Attack de Vive Force, Surprise 108
Bombardment, Blockades 110
Siege 111

Sec. II. SIEGE 112
Investment 112
Selection of the Point of Attack 113
First Parallel 115

PAGE

Opening of the Trenches 118
Batteries 119
Second Parallel, Flying Sap 121
Defence 123

Sec. III. SIEGE 125
Demi-Parallels 125
Sap and Double Sap 126
Third Parallel 127
Circular Portions, Crowning of the Covered Way, Cavalier
    Trenches 128
Breaching Batteries and Counter Batteries 131
Descent into the Ditch 132
Assault 134
Defence 135

CHAPTER VII.

Sec. I. SYSTEMS OF VAUBAN 139
Analysis of the First System 139
Second System 145
Third System 146

Sec. II. MODERN SYSTEM 147
Tracing 147
Profiles 148
Details 155

Sec. III. ADDITIONAL WORKS 157
Interior Retrenchments 157
Hornworks, Tenaillons 158
Counterguards 159
Citadels, Retrenched Camps 161
Water, Mines, and Counter-Mines 163
Globe of Compression 165
Camouflet 166

Chapter VIII.

		PAGE
Of Different Systems		167
Italian System		167
Spanish System		168
Dutch System.		168
Errard de Bar-le-Duc		169
Chevalier de Ville		170
Count Pagan		170
Vauban		171
Coëhorn		172
Bousmard		174
Chasseloup Laubat		176
Dufour		177
Montalembert		177
Carnot		178
German System		180
Remarks on Systems		182
Choumara		184
Remarks on the Ideas of Choumara		188

Chapter IX.

Besieging Army and Garrison		191
Force of a Besieging Army		191
Strength of a Garrison		194
Amount of Artillery necessary for the Defence		195
Amount of Artillery necessary for the Attack		196

Chapter X.

Fortifications for the Defence of a Country		198

xii   CONTENTS.

APPENDIX.

                                                              PAGE
Note I.   PENETRATION OF PROJECTILES 207
Note II. DIMENSIONS OF REDOUBTS 211
Note III. CALCULATION OF THE EQUALITY OF DEBLAI AND
          REMBLAI 215
Note IV. 220

FORTIFICATION.

CHAPTER I.

DEFINITIONS.

(1) *Fortification* is employed for the purpose of enabling a body of men to resist with advantage the attack of a greater force.

It is either *Natural* or *Artificial.*

A chain of mountains, the sea, a river, are natural fortifications; whilst any work made by the hand of man is artificial. To the latter only we shall direct our attention.

It has been divided into *Permanent* and *Temporary,* or *Field Fortification.* As the name implies, permanent works are intended to stand for ages, as those that surround arsenals, frontier places; whilst fieldworks are thrown up merely for a time, to occupy or defend a position, protect a bridge or a village.

(2) It ought never to be lost sight of that in every description of warfare fortification is only an accessory, destined to increase the power of resistance of troops; and that works, particularly in the field, are only resorted to when we are weaker than our adversary. Fortification

B

should not, therefore, paralyse the action of the troops, as has too often been the case, but give full scope to their efficacy.

Cavalry can only act offensively; infantry and artillery can act both on the offensive and the defensive, and for the latter alone is fortification employed. It should at the same time protect them, and enable them to concentrate their fire so as to give it its fullest effect, conditions concisely expressed by a celebrated engineer, 'it must *cover and flank.*' To these we might add, it must also *make the most of the ground,* for in fortification more still than in tactics, it is true that bravery is worth more than numbers; but the nature of the ground is often of more use than bravery.

Sec. I.   ON FIRING.

(3) Fieldworks, as well as permanent works, are constructed in such a manner as to be defensible by musketry alone. It is true that artillery is often employed in the field, and constantly so in fortresses; but although it is always useful, and increases the power of resistance, yet it cannot always be had when required, whilst soldiers constantly carry their muskets.

For the intelligence of the principles hereafter developed, the student should be familiar with the various names given to the fire of guns and muskets, according to its direction and nature.

(4) *Direct Fire* (1), when the projectile strikes perpendicularly the outside of a work, or the front of a troop.

(5) *Oblique Fire* (2), when it strikes in an oblique direction.

(6) *Enfilade Fire* (3), when it is directed on the flank of a troop from one end to another, or along the banquette (16) or rampart of a work.

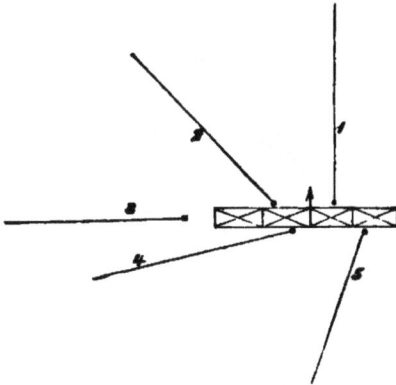

Fig. 1.

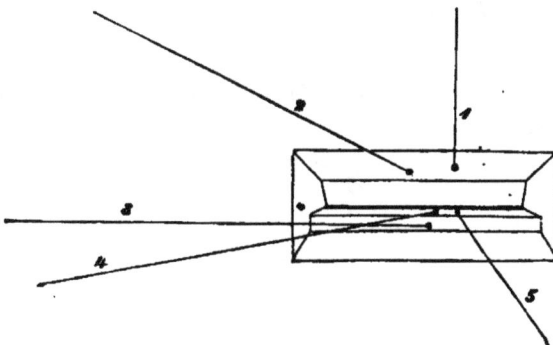

(7) *Slanting Fire* (4), when it strikes the rear of a troop, or the interior of a work, at a small angle.

(8) *Reverse Fire* (5), when this angle is larger.

(9) When two faces of a work, or of different works, are so disposed that the fire of one face can defend the ground in front of the other, we say that the space *A* is exposed to *cross fire,*

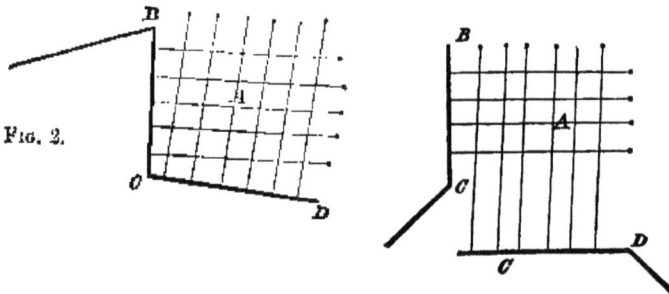

Fig. 2.

and that the face *BC* flanks the face *CD*, and conversely that the face *CD* flanks the face *BC*.

If a ditch is defended by a work in the rear, the ditch is said to be *flanked.*

(10) We may still mention *Vertical Fire*, that of a mortar.

Fig. 3.

(11) *Ricochet Fire*, that of a gun or howitzer, fired at a small angle, and with a small charge of powder, the shot bounding along as in this diagram :—

Fig. 4.

It is chiefly employed for the enfilade; it was discovered by Vauban, and used for the first time at the siege of Ath in 1697.

(12) *Pitching Fire*, when the shot is projected against a work to be destroyed, which is covered in front by another work.

Fig. 5.

(13) *Plunging Fire*, when it comes from a commanding position.

Fig. 6.

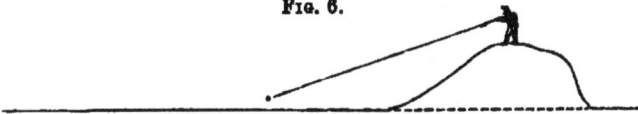

Sec. II.   DITCH AND COVERING MASS.

(14) Fortification is the most ancient of all the arts of war; nature itself has pointed it out to us. The first man attacked by an enemy stronger than himself, in the consciousness of his inferiority, sought a remedy for it. A

bush, a rock, a trunk of a tree must have served him as a fortification. To the present day we find savages possessed of no other, and we ourselves employ this primitive fortification in partial and sudden attacks. The natural hedge led us to the idea of forming artificial ones or abattis, the rock taught us to construct walls, and the ravine a parapet made of the earth extracted from a ditch. This kind of fortification protected the first houses against the attacks of wild beasts, and afterwards against men.*

(15) Let us suppose a body of men in the open country threatened by a superior force, the first idea that will present itself will undoubtedly be to find a means to stop its advance : a *ditch* will answer this purpose.

FIG. 7.

Still the superiority of number will soon tell by a more deadly fire ; a cover is therefore necessary, and if the earth extracted from the ditch is thrown up in a heap, the men will become comparatively safe.

FIG. 8.

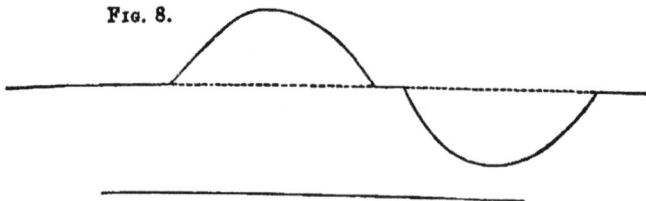

* *Encyclopédie*, Diderot.

Yet, if they remain inactive behind such a mask, the enemy would soon overcome the obstacle; but if this *covering mass* is constructed in such a way as to allow of the defenders firing over it, then the attacking party becomes exposed, and the inequality of number partially remedied. All fortification consists thus of two distinct parts, a ditch and a covering mass.

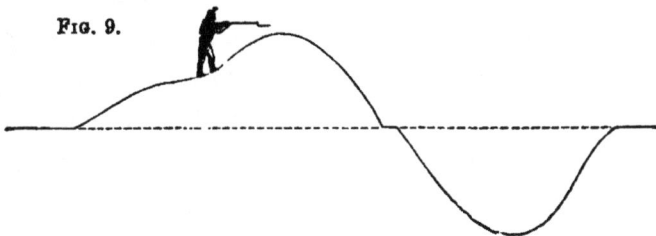

Fig. 9.

(16) The earth extracted from the ditch would not resist projectiles, and would soon be penetrated by rain and scattered by wind, if it were not rammed in and shaped regularly.

In the annexed diagram we give the representation of the covering mass, as it is now constructed.

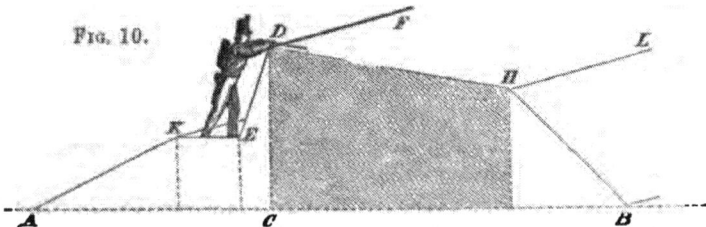

Fig. 10.

The line *AB* figures the surface of the ground. The part shaded is called the *Parapet* (from the Italian, *para* *petto,* covering the chest). Its thickness varies according to the weapons at the disposal of the assailant, from 3 to 18 feet. Its standard height *CD* is 8 feet.*

The *superior slope†* *DH* slants towards the country, with an inclination ⅔, in order to enable the defenders to fire immediately in front. These are posted on the *Banquette KE*. It is level or slightly inclined to the rear, to carry off the water; it is 3 feet wide, or 4 ft. 6 in. when destined for two files of men, and stands 4 ft. 3 in. below the *Crest** of the Parapet, this being the most convenient height for a man to fire over and remain at the same time covered. To ascend from the interior of the work, or *Terreplein,* up

---

* See Appendix, Note 1.

† In Fortification, the inclination of a slope is obtained by dividing its base by its height, it being much easier on the ground to measure lengths than angles. Thus, if the base is equal to 2 yards, and the height 1 yard, we say that the slope is ½. If the base is 3 yards, and the height 3 yards, the slope is ⅓. If the base is 1 ft., and the height 4 ft., the slope is ¼, &c.

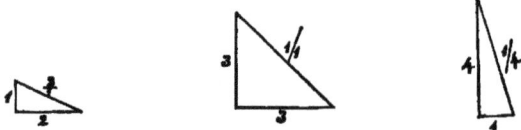

A slope ⅓ is also called a slope at 45°; it is the natural inclination earth will take when left to itself.

‡ The highest line (*DF*) of a parapet is called the *Interior Crest;* the lower (*HL*), the *Exterior Crest*. The former is also named the *Line of Fire,* because it is from it that the fire is poured out; the Superior Slope is, in the same manner, called the *Plane of Fire.* (Fig. 4.)

to the Banquette, a *Slope of Banquette AK* at ¾ is constructed.

The Parapet is connected with the Banquette by the *Interior Slope DE*, at ⅓, and with the ground on the outside by the *Exterior Slope HB* at ¼.

In Field Fortification this shape is constant.

In Permanent Fortification we find also a *Rampart AB* or large mass of earth of various heights, and its *slope of Rampart AC*, at ¼.

Fɪɢ. 11.

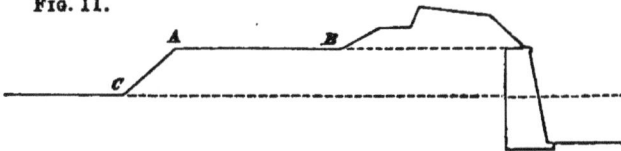

This additional height is necessary to protect the buildings, and to command the country.

(17) The height of the Parapet is called the *Relief;* in comparing several works the difference of Relief is called the *Command.* Thus, the work *A* has a command of 4 feet on the work *B.* The relief of *A* is 12 feet, that of *B* 8 feet.

Fɪɢ. 12.

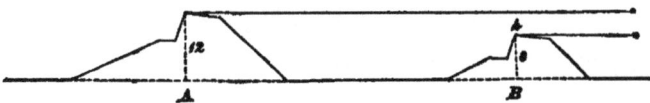

The standard height of a work is 8 feet; in some instances it may be raised to 12, but never above; and it may also be lowered to 7, or even $6\frac{1}{2}$. When the relief is great it is called a *Bold Relief;* when below 8 ft. a *Low Relief.*

(18) *The Ditch* is comprised between two slopes; that next to the Parapet *AB* is called the *Escarp;* that towards the country *CD*, the *Counterscarp;* the level part *BD* is the bottom.

Fɪɢ. 13.

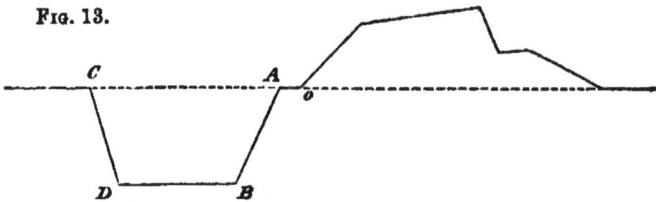

The inclination of the scarps varies according to the nature of the soil, from $\frac{1}{1}$ to $\frac{1}{3}$;* but the escarp, having to support all the covering mass, is always made less steep than the counterscarp; and, to diminish this enormous pressure, a horizontal space *Ao*, called a *Berm*, is reserved at the foot of the exterior slope. It varies from 1 to 3 feet, according to the nature of the ground; but it is an inconvenience, and must be avoided when possible, because it affords a resting-place for the assailants, who, after having

	Escarp.	Counterscarp.	Berm.
* Strong soil	$\frac{1}{3}$	$\frac{1}{3}$	1 f.
Ordinary soil	$\frac{1}{2}$	$\frac{1}{2}$	2 f.
Sandy soil	$\frac{1}{1}$	$\frac{1}{1}$	3 f.

cleared the ditch, gather in sufficient numbers to give the assault. At the attack of the tête-de-pont of Almaraz, made by the English in the Peninsula (1812), the berms of Fort Napoleon kept off the ends of the scaling-ladders from the parapet; but the first men jumped on to the berm itself, and, drawing up the ladders, planted them there; then, with a second escalade, they won the work.

In Permanent Fortification these slopes are generally built in masonry, and are either ⅕th, as in Vauban, or perpendicular, as in the Modern System.

When a slope is steeper than ½, earth must be supported by masonry, sandbags, sods, &c. This is called Revetment.

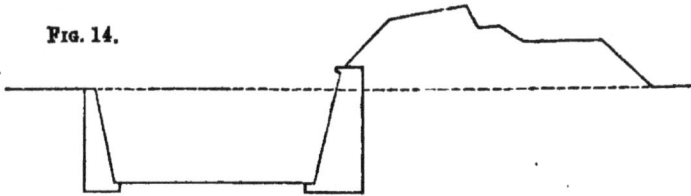

Fig. 14.

(19) The *depth* of a Ditch in Field Fortification varies from 8 to 12 ft.; below 8 ft. it would no longer be a serious obstacle; above 12 it would become too difficult to excavate.

The *width* is never less than 12 feet, but may extend to 20, or even 25, feet.

In Permanent works the depth may average 30 feet, and even more, and the width 90 feet and upwards.

(20) It is a principle that is constantly adhered to, espe-

cially in the field, that the ditch must furnish all the earth necessary for the covering mass. Therefore, when the thickness of the Parapet has been once determined upon, one may assume the depth of the ditch (8 ft. or 12 ft.), and calculate the width, or assume the width (never less than 12 ft.), and calculate the depth. This operation is called the calculation of *deblai* (ditch), and *remblai* (mass).

(21) The critical moment for the assailant is the instant when he arrives at the counterscarp of the ditch, because he hesitates to cross it, and is there exposed to a murderous fire; but if the parapet is small, and the ditch narrow, the superior slope produced meets the ground too far, and a man might stand safely at *A*. To obviate this the ground is raised as in *CB*, and this double slope is called a *Glacis*.

Fig. 15.

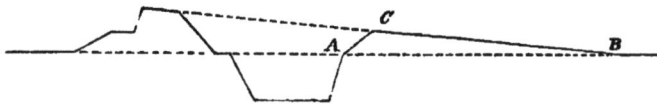

(22) Finally, to complete the work, a little path is sometimes reserved between the Counterscarp and the Glacis. It is called a *Covered Way*.

Fig. 16.

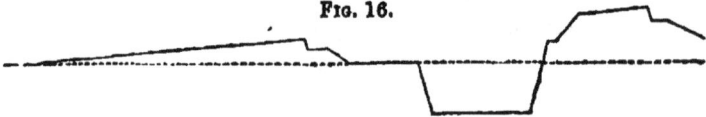

It is rarely employed in Field Fortification, but is constantly to be found in Permanent Fortification.

The two component parts of all Fortification are the Parapet and the Ditch; in its more complicated state we find the Rampart, Parapet, Ditch, Glacis, and Covered Way.

Sec. III.   OUTLINE.

(23) A parapet and a ditch that would stretch along the ground in a straight line would not completely answer the purpose in view, since the defenders could only oppose a direct fire to a superior one, and this defence would cease as soon as the assailant is in the ditch.

It is necessary to construct the work according to a crooked line, offering *salient*, *AAA*, and *re-entering* angles, *BBB*. By this disposition the assailant is exposed to fire in several directions, and he will be compelled to abstain from attacking the re-entering angles in order to direct his efforts on the salients, where he is less exposed. The defenders give thus a superiority to their musketry, and can concentrate their means of resistance where they are likely to be attacked.

Fig. 17.

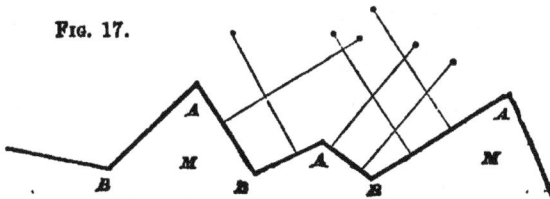

The Parapet and Ditch being thus constructed along faces, enclose a space *M*, and form what is called an *Intrenchment*.*

The combination of these angles, and the general configuration of the work on the ground, constitute what is called the *Outline*, or *Trace*.

This outline will vary indefinitely, and it is in its judicious selection that an officer will display his skill, it being borne in mind that Fortification must make the best of the ground.

In representing Fortification on paper, it is usual to give the outline, together with the dimensions of the parapet and ditch ; with these two elements we can judge of a work, and pronounce on its intrinsic value.

(24) In the drawing of a plan of a field-work (Fig. 18), the lines *AB* represent the *line of fire*. In that of a permanent work (Fig. 19) it is the top of the scarp, and is called the *Master-line*. This line is always strongly marked in the drawing.

(25) The figure giving the dimensions of the ditch and parapet is called a *Profile*. This figure results, as is seen by the diagram, from the intersection of the work by a plane. It is either *Right*, as in *RR*, or *Oblique*, as in *CD*, accord-

---

* *Epaulment* differs from an Intrenchment by the absence of the banquette and its slope. It is constructed for the purpose of Artillery.

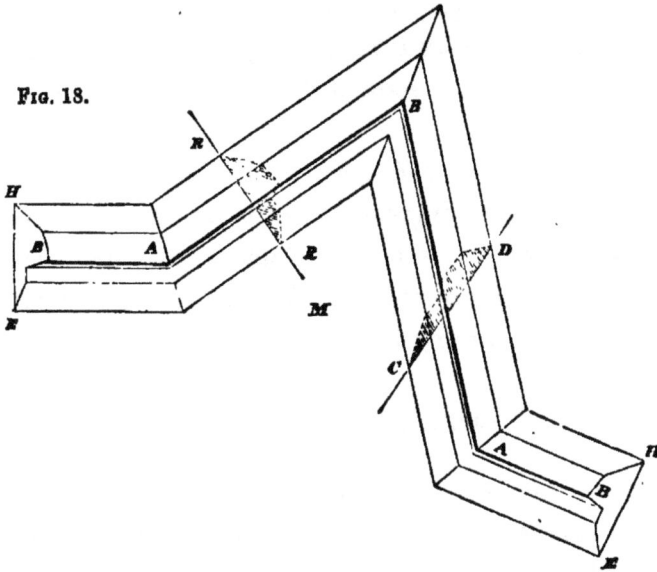

Fig. 18.

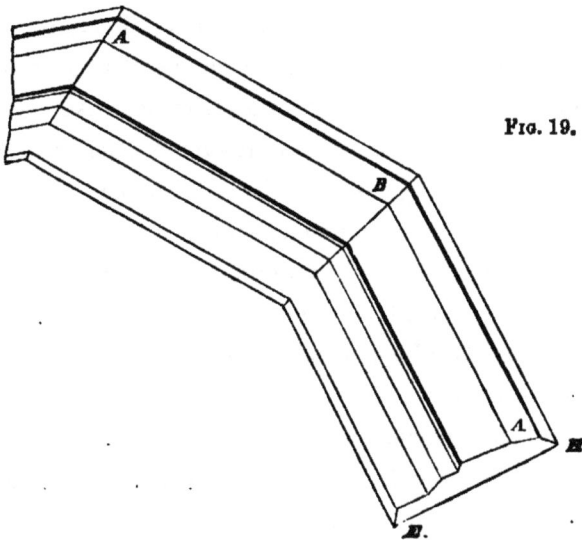

Fig. 19.

ing as the plan is perpendicular or oblique to the line of fire. *Extreme Profiles* is the name given to the slope that, like *EH*, supports the earth at the extremity of a face.

(26) The Outline and the Profile completely define a work. When the Parapet is thick, we say that it is a work of Strong Profile; when the Salients and Re-entering Angles offer a good combination for the defence, we say that it is a good or a Strong Outline.

Sec. IV. PROPERTIES OF THE OUTLINE.

(27) To understand the properties of angles, it must be observed that a soldier behind a parapet is expected to fire straight before him, and that unless he is expressly ordered to do so, he must not fire in an oblique direction. This rule is most essential. It often happens that a troop is called upon to occupy and defend a series of works, the outline of which is calculated to answer a combination of defence. The flanking of a ditch or of a face *must* take place: it is a sacred duty, and a garrison must even sacrifice its safety to fulfil it, as a rearguard or an outpost must sometimes devote itself for the safety of the army.

If, then, we consider a salient angle, the shots of the last man on each face leave a space totally *undefended*. (Fig. 20.) This is an inconvenience common to all salient angles, and is another reason which will induce the assailant to select the salient as the point of attack.

The smaller the angle, the larger will be this undefended space; besides, with a very acute angle, the parapets of

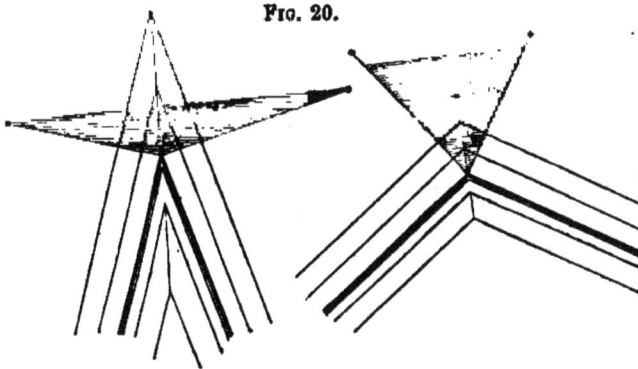

FIG. 20.

both faces would meet on a narrow ridge, unable to resist the fire of the enemy's artillery, or even heavy rains ; and the interior space would become so limited that no room would be left for a gun in the capital,* a measure often adopted to send fire on the advancing columns of attack.

For these reasons the salient angles must never be less than 60°.†

(28) In a re-entering angle, as well as in any two faces flanking each other, we find an inconvenience of a similar sort. The superior slope of the parapet being $\frac{6}{1}$, the ditch

---

* The line that bisects a salient angle is called in Fortification its *Capital*.

† Angles are usually measured in the field by means of lines; a simple method to obtain an angle of 60° is to form an equilateral tri-

cannot be seen by the defender, in the whole part shaded; once arrived there, the enemy is safe. This space is called a *dead angle*.

FIG. 21.

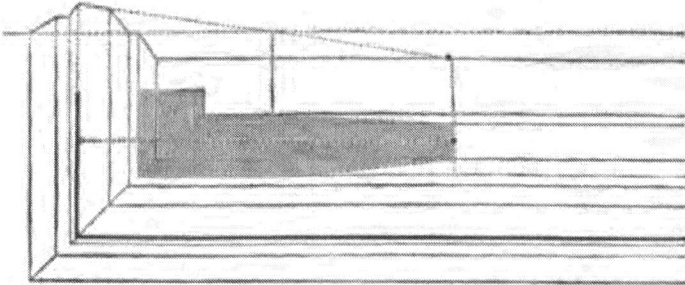

With regard to the re-entering angle, we have seen that its faces are intended to cross their fire, and to flank each other. Should the angle be small, the men would shoot on their own party; should it be very large, the flanking could not be effected but by an oblique fire. Therefore, limits have been fixed from 90° to 120° for these angles.

---

angle with three equal pieces of string. A right angle, 90°, is also obtained by making a right-angled triangle with three strings of length respectively 3, 4, and 5.

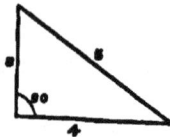

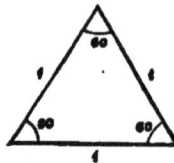

FIG. 22.

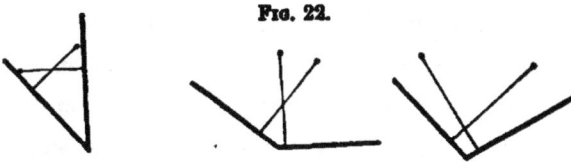

(29) *Dimensions of Faces.*—Salients are points of attack: we obviate the inconvenience of the undefended space which they necessarily present by artillery in the capital, by accessory means, and, above all, by flanking. The critical moment is when the enemy arrives at the counterscarp and descends into the ditch; should he then be unexposed, he may mine the work, or collect in sufficient force to assault it vigorously. We have seen that along every face flanked,

FIG. 23.

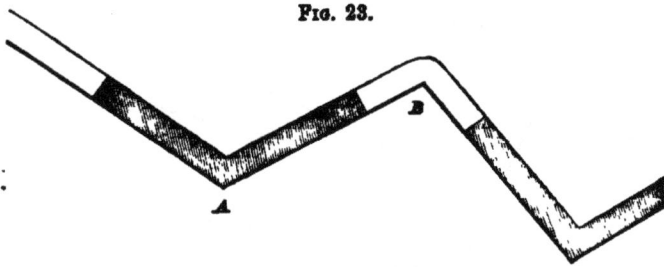

AB, there is a dead angle, occupying nearly 30 yards; if the faces then are shorter than 30 yards, no part of the ditch is seen by the defenders. As, however, the enemy in reaching the salient *B* must be seen in the ditch, we are obliged to make the faces longer than 30 yards.

Although musketry carries as far as 250 yards, a face *AB* could not be made of that length, because the shots

c 2

reaching the salient would become very uncertain. The
greatest distance at which a flanking fire of musketry can
be relied on should not exceed 180 yards, and even faces
ought not, if possible, to exceed 100 yards. In permanent
fortification this rule may be modified in some particular
instances, where artillery can always be employed, and the
distance of flanking extended to 200 yards. These limits

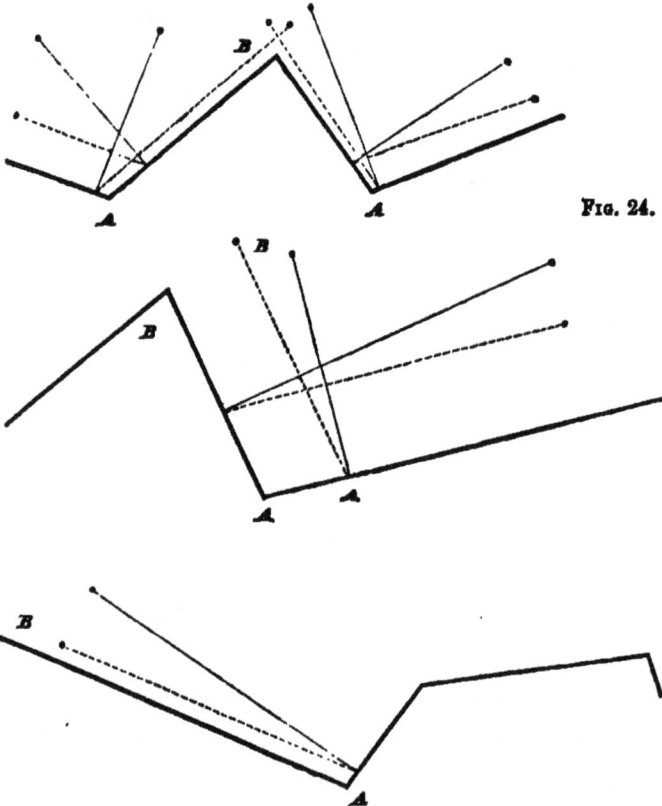

Fig. 24.

are based upon the range of the old musket. The introduction of the Minié rifle in the army will permit an increase of the length of the faces from 180 to 600 yards distance, at which the practice of this new weapon can be relied upon. It will not affect field fortification beyond the necessity of extending the defilade (85) of a work to a greater distance, but in permanent fortification it will permit the extension of the fronts (40), an improvement much insisted upon by modern engineers.

The sides of a re-entering angle, according to the direction of which a face is flanked, are called *lines of defence*: such are *AB, AB*: and the angle *A*, an *angle of defence.* (Fig. 24.)

(30) The fundamental principles of all fortification which we now recapitulate, have been deduced from the nature of the arms employed, and are rendered evident by the most simple considerations.

The extent of a work must be proportioned to the number of men intended for its defence.

The outline must give as much direct and flanking fire to bear on the point of attack as possible.

The salient angles must never be less than 60°.

The angle of defence must be between 90° and 120°.

The lines of defence must be smaller than 180°.

A work in which all these conditions are observed is called a good work, but here theory must give way before practice: the ground to fortify is given, and we must make the best of the foregoing principles; but it is not always possible to apply them all at the same time. Although in theory a work without flanking is deficient, yet the conformation of the ground and the destination of the work may be such, that this consideration becomes of less importance, and the work is nevertheless a good work.

CHAPTER II.

Sec. I. NOMENCLATURE OF FIELD-WORKS.

(31) The profile of a field-work has already been given
(Fig. 10). It has been shown that its standard height is
8 feet; and that the other dimensions are dependent upon
the weight of the enemy's metal and the nature of the soil.
The outlines of this sort of work vary *ad infinitum,* but we
may classify them under two heads, *Isolated works,* and
combined works or *Lines.* The former are subdivided into
open and *enclosed* works; the latter into *Continued Lines,*
and *Lines with intervals.*

(32) *Open Works.*—Under this category we place all the
works opened at the rear or *Gorge,* and we may bring them
to three types, which are, as it were, the element of an
infinity of others.

1st. The *Redan,* formed of two faces salient towards the
enemy.

Fig. 25.

2nd. The *Lunette*, formed of two faces and two flanks.

Fig. 26.

3rd. The *Tenaille*, formed of two faces, presenting a re-entering angle to the assailant.

Fig. 27.

Among the many works derived from them, few have received a special name.

The *Double Redan*.

Fig. 28.

The *Tenaille Head*.

Fig. 29.

The *Queue d'Hironde*, or swallow's tail.

Fig. 30.

The *Bonnet de Prêtre.*

Fig. 31.

All these may be somewhat modified, especially to obtain flanking fire, and they still retain their names; thus—

Fig. 32.

Fig. 33.

Fig. 34.

A, A, A, are still called redans.

The name of *Hornworks,* or Bastion-head, applies in general to all works composed of a bastioned front and two faces.

Fig. 35.

Fig. 36.

That of *Crown Works* to open works containing more than a bastioned front.

Fig. 37.

When any one of these works is employed to defend a bridge, it is called a Bridge-head—Tête-de-Pont in French.

(33) A mere inspection of these figures, shows the defects of these outlines when employed by themselves. Thus the Redan and Lunette have no flank defence, and the ground before the salients is deprived of fire. The Tenaille has flanking fire, but its ditch contains a dead angle.

We may here observe, that although these works have by themselves but a weak outline, they are, nevertheless, capable of making a most vigorous resistance when flanked by others in the rear; the inconveniences we have alluded to are besides, as we shall hereafter see, obviated by accessory means, artillery, obstacles, &c. The redans at Sebastopol in 1855, will not easily be forgotten.

(34) *Enclosed Works.*—Here, again, we have three different types—the Redoubt, the Star-fort or fortlet, and the Fort.

A *Redoubt* is an enclosed work having no re-entering angle, and is formed of 4, 5, or 6 faces, but generally of 4. It may even be circular.

FIG. 38.   FIG. 39.   FIG. 40.   FIG. 41.

A *Star-fort* presents a series of salient and re-entering angles; the number of salients may be 4, 5, 6, 8, &c.

Fig. 42.   Fig. 43.   Fig. 44.   Fig. 45.   Fig. 46.

A *Fort* is the name given to any enclosed work possessing bastions (40); it may be Square or Pentagonal.

Fig. 47.   Fig. 48.

 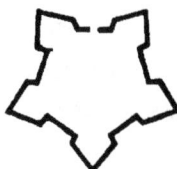

(35) These outlines, again, can be immediately appreciated: the Redoubt, with its unflanked ditches and its undefended angles, is not capable of a good defence by itself: the Star-forts appear better, but the greater part of their ditches is dead; their enclosed space is small for the long extent of their parapet, and their faces are exposed to enfilade. The Forts are the best, as will be seen, when the Bastion is treated of.* This, again, is true, when we suppose these works to be placed under the same conditions, in

---

* No. 40.

a plain for instance, but military history gives us instances of the great value of works having of themselves but a weak outline. Thus, at Montenotte, in 1796, a redoubt, garrisoned with 1500 French Grenadiers, resisted successfully during a day and a night the repeated attacks of 12,000 Austrians. The redoubt of the Stamboul gate at Silistria, in 1854, stood the continuous attacks of the Russians.

The redoubts established in 1855, at Kars, by Colonel Lake, owing to their skilful disposition and mutual flanking, resisted during months the efforts of the Russians.

(36) Among the enclosed works we may place the *Blockhouses*; these are employed in woody and mountainous countries where timber abounds, and where artillery is not likely to attack them. Their outline varies; the Square

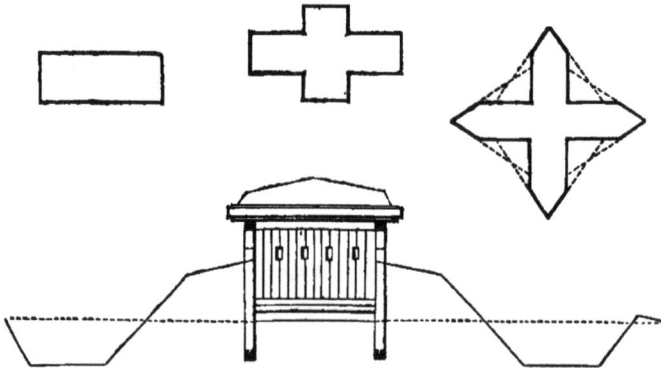

Fig. 49.

and the Cross being the most general forms. The walls are formed of logs of wood from 9 to 12 inches square, buried 3 ft., connected to sills and cap-sills, the latter consolidated by girders. The interior should be 20 ft. wide, and 9 high in the clear. Loopholes are pierced 3 ft. apart, and a banquette, serving as a campbed, allows the men to fire through them. A parapet of earth and a ditch prevent the access of the enemy.

When artillery can be brought against these works, their wall is made of two rows of logs, the space between the timber being filled up with earth well rammed in.

Fig. 50.

The profile of their walls varies much.

The roof is covered with earth 3 ft. thick to avoid fire, and render it bombproof, and is sometimes furnished with a banquette.

Sometimes the blockhouse has two stories. (See Fig. 51.) They make good defensive barracks in a hostile country.

Blockhouses were erected in 1849, in the bastions (40) of Vienna, commanding the principal streets, as a defence against future internal enemies in the Austrian capital.

Fig. 51.

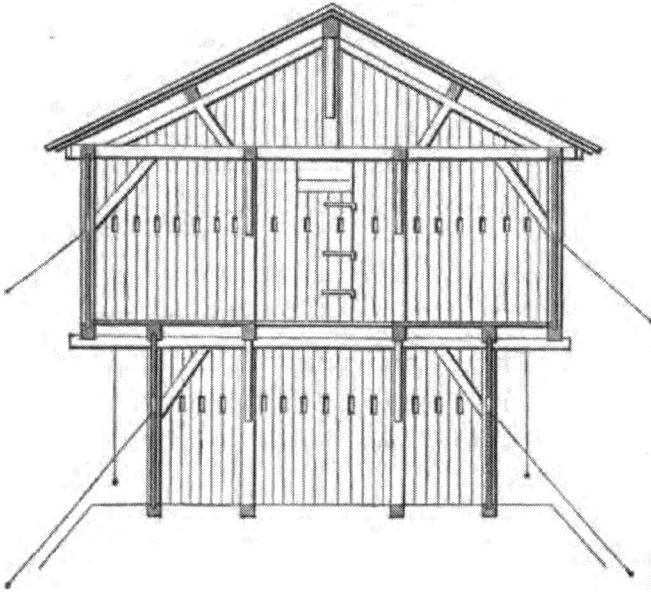

(37) *Lines.*—This is the name given to the intrench-ments constructed to fortify the position of an army, or to connect important forts or redoubts. According to their object, they are called *Intrenched Positions, Intrenched Camps, Lines of Circumvallation, Lines of Contravalla-tion,* but the two latter are obsolete.

With regard to their arrangement, they either cover the ground without interruption, or are composed of works com-bined for a common defence; in the first case they are called Continued Lines, in the latter, Lines with Intervals.

(38) *Continued Lines.*—These are to be avoided, on

account of the amount of labour they require, which bears
no proportion to their value; in fact, the defenders may
expect an attack on every point and prepare for it, whether
real or false, and once the line is forced at a point, it is
altogether lost. They have but an historical interest. The
chief sorts are—

The *Tenaille Lines*.

FIG. 52.

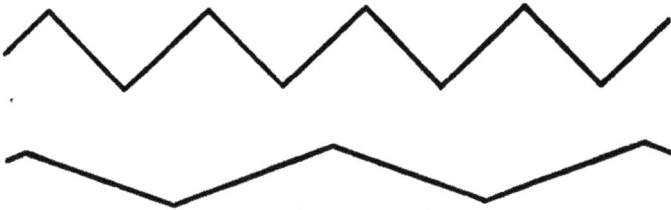

The *Lines of Vauban* or *Redan Lines*, with small or
large Redans.

FIG. 53.

Continued Redan Lines.

FIG. 54.

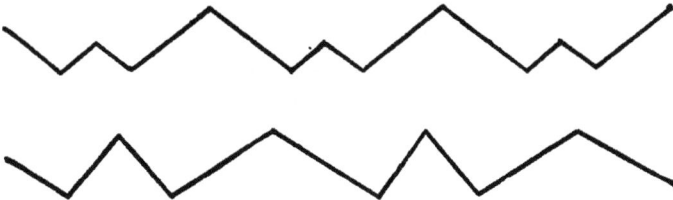

Indented Lines.

FIG. 55.

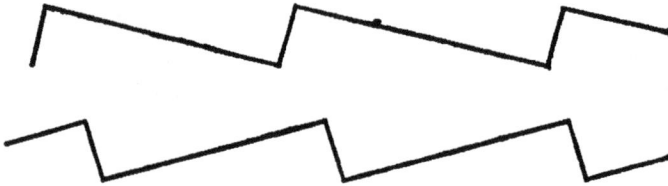

Bastioned Lines.

FIG. 56.

(39) *Lines with Intervals.*—These are formed of detached works, placed at such intervals as to derive protection from one another, and so as to cross their fire on the intervening space. Different outlines may be selected, two or three rows of lunettes, or two or three rows of redoubts.

FIG. 57.

FIG. 58.

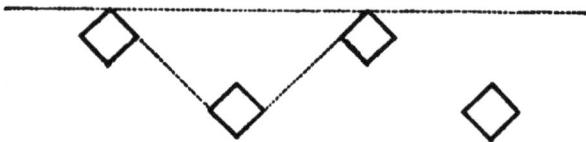

Such lines can more easily be adapted to the ground, and occasion less labour; they permit the defenders to move rapidly and in force on the intervals to repel the attack, and assume the offensive when the opportunity presents itself; an immense advantage over the Continued Lines, where the defensive attitude is compulsory.

During the seventeenth and even the eighteenth century, continued lines were frequently employed to cover an army engaged in besieging a fortress, or to defend a position; but experience has rendered us wiser: we no longer employ them in a siege, and we have recourse to the lines with intervals whenever we require to defend a position of some extent.

At Arras, in 1634, Turenne made three false attacks on the lines constructed by Condé and the Archduke Leopold, and succeeded in forcing them.

In 1656, at Valenciennes, the lines of Turenne were also forced by Condé.

In 1706, at Turin, Prince Eugene defeated Marsin, who awaited him behind his lines.

In 1793, the Prince of Cobourg, commanding the Austrian forces (60,000 men), was attacked in his lines at Wattignies, by General Jourdan, at the head of 40,000 French troops, and was compelled to raise the blockade of Maubeuge.

It was during the Seven Years' War that the Prussians and Austrians had recourse to powerful combinations of lines with intervals. The most remarkable were those of the King of Prussia, near Jauernig; those of H.R.H. Prince

Henry, near Liebenthal, in 1759; those at Colberg, in 1761; and those of the Austrians at Dippoldiswalde, in 1759; at Boxdorff, in 1761; and upon the high Eulengebürge, in 1762. In the Peninsular war the most celebrated were those constructed at Torres Vedras, by the Duke of Wellington, in 1810.

(40) *Of Bastions.*—The serious inconvenience of dead angles has rendered it advisable to adopt a combination of such a kind that in no part of the ditch should a man be sheltered from the fire of the defenders. The bastioned outline, discovered three hundred years ago, for permanent works, completely answers this purpose, and is advantageously employed in Field Fortification.

Let us suppose that a work of that kind is to be constructed to defend a position, and let us take the case of a square fort.

The lines $AB, BD, DC, CA,$ are called *fronts,* and for each of them the construction is the same.

On the middle of the line $AB,$ a perpendicular $CD,$ called the *Perpendicular* of the front, is drawn; and towards the interior, a length CD is taken, equal to ⅛th of the front. Join AD and BD; on these two lines measure the distances BE and $AB,$ equal to ⅔ths of the front; from H draw HK perpendicular to $KB,$ and from E, EM perpendicular to $MA.$ Join $KM,$ and $AHKMEB$ will be the outline of the bastioned front, which consists of two half bastions and a *Curtain KM.*

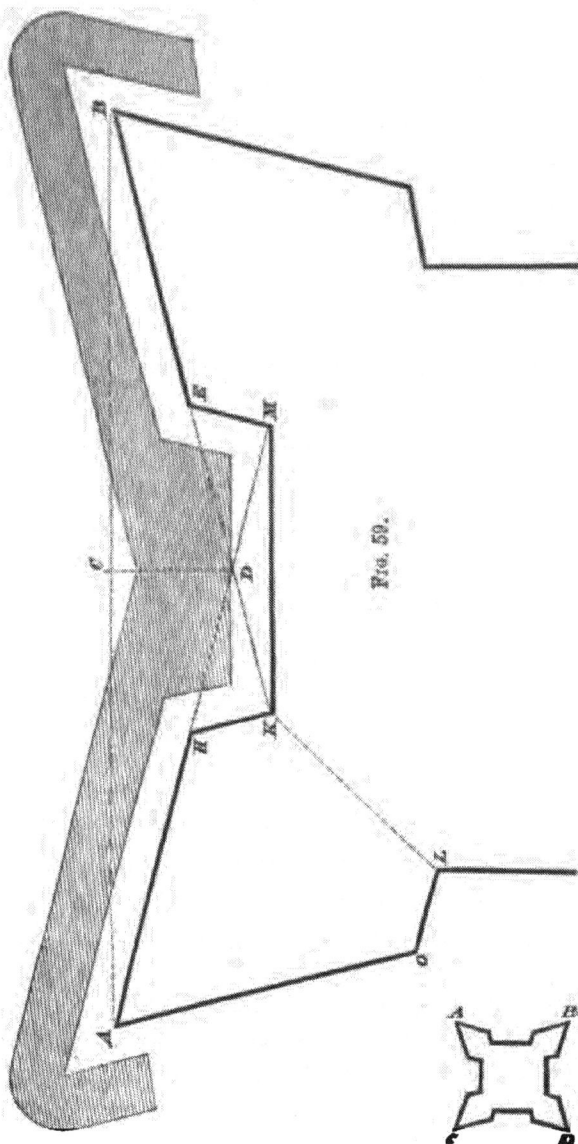

Fig. 59.

The same construction being repeated thus on each front, a *Bastion** *KHAOL* will consist of two half-bastions.

The lines *HK, EM*, are called *flanks; AH, BE*, are called *faces; KL* the gorge of a bastion; *AM, BK, Lines of defence*. The angles at *A, B*, are Salient or *Flanked Angles*, the angles *K, M*, are called the *Angles of the Flank*, those at *H, E, Shoulder Angles*.

In inspecting this outline, it will be perceived that at whatever point the enemy presents himself, he is exposed to cross fire in several directions ; and that if *DM* is greater than 30 yds., there is no longer a dead angle ; to increase this advantage, the counterscarp is not kept parallel to the line of fire of the curtain, but the ditch is excavated, as in the shaded figure. Every part of the ditch is thus seen by the defenders, half by the flank *ME*, half by the flank *HK*. This condition of making *DM* greater than 30 yds. gives for the relief of field-works the minimum of 200 yds. ; and as the lines of defence should not exceed 180 or 200 yds., the greatest front we should take is about 300 yds.

The length of the perpendicular, fixed at $\frac{1}{8}$th of the front for the square, is made $\frac{1}{7}$th for the pentagon, and $\frac{1}{6}$th for figures of a greater number of sides.

In Lines the general front is subdivided into partial fronts

---

* This word comes from the Italian 'bastido,' a tower; bastions made of earth were invented to replace in Permanent Fortification the tower that flanked the walls of a town, after the discovery of gunpowder and the use of artillery.

(Fig. 56), and the same construction as above is adopted. In Hornworks and Crownworks the method is also the same.

The perpendicular which is fixed for enclosed works, in order to give to the salient angles an opening greater than 60°, varies here, according to circumstances, from $\frac{1}{8}$th to $\frac{1}{15}$th.

Sec. II. SELECTION OF AN OUTLINE.

(41) The ground is the first element to be considered before selecting a particular outline, but it is not the only one : we must also bear in mind the end for which the work is designed, and the force of the garrison destined for its defence. Again, the amount of labour, and the time required to throw up the work, may further induce us to modify this outline.

With regard to the Ground, and the Purpose of the work, no absolute rule can be laid down; here all is left to the ingenuity of the officer, and none should ever forget that it is not by difficult and complicated tracings that he will display his skill.

If a bridge thrown across a river is to be defended by a work, the figure shows that a redan would not answer the

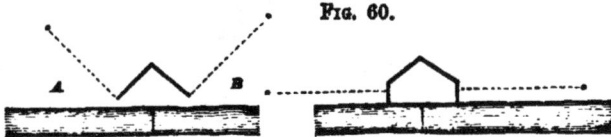

Fig. 60.

purpose if the river run in a straight line; the assailant being in fact unexposed in his approach on the ground *A* and *B;* this outline would, on the contrary, be good when the river presents sinuosities; the lunette should be preferred on the first supposition.

FIG. 61.

If a marsh or ground impassable to the enemy is in the vicinity of a position, it would be absurd to place a face parallel to the obstacle, since its fire would be lost; on the contrary, in directing a salient towards it, we at once obviate the disadvantage of the want of fire on the capital.

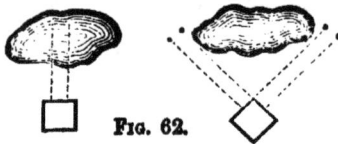

FIG. 62.

If a work must be thrown up close to a commanding height, the outlines 1, 2, 3, would give faces exposed to enfilade and reverse fire; the outline 4 should be preferred.

Fig. 63.

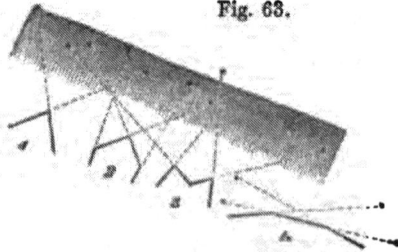

If the work is to be constructed in a valley between two commanding heights, outline 1 would again be absurd, so would be any other but figure 2.

FIG. 64.

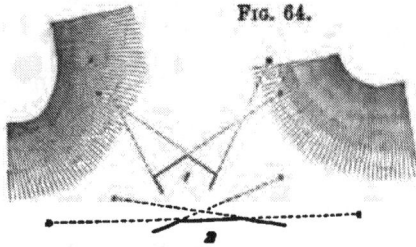

Again, the redoubt 1 has all its faces exposed to enfilade and reverse fire, while redoubt 2 has better conditions.

FIG. 65.

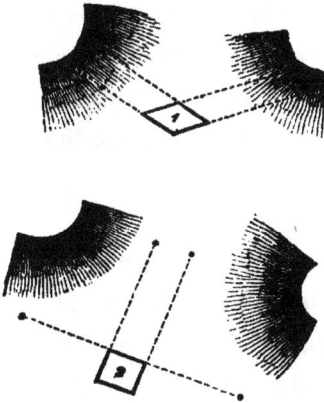

FIG. 66.

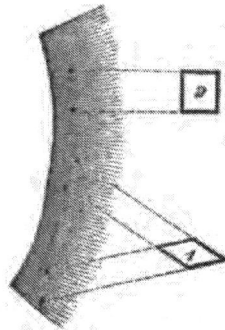

Examples of this kind could be multiplied *ad infinitum*, but a perusal of former campaigns is the best exercise that can be recommended to an officer desirous, in time of peace,

of acquiring information, if not experience, on this important
subject.

(42) To fix the strength of a *garrison,* it is usual to
compute two men for every yard of the crest of the parapet
in open works :—thus, a Redan destined for 80 men should
have 40 yards of parapet. Besides the men stationed on
the banquette, a reserve is placed on the terreplein ; it is
generally a third of the whole garrison.

If a lunette having 90 yards of parapet is to be
garrisoned, the detachment should muster 270, 180 on
the banquette, 90 forming reserves.

If two files of men be judged necessary for a good
defence, the garrison should be calculated in the same
manner: 360 for the banquette, 180 for the reserves. The
same data will serve for lines; but as these are defended ·
by large armies, the calculation need not be very exact,
inasmuch as there is a sufficient number of men to line the
banquette in one, two, or three files.

(43) When the work is an enclosed one, the terreplein
must afford sufficient accommodation to the defenders for
bivouacking, and its surface must enter into this calculation, 15 square feet being allowed for every man. The
dimensions of enclosed works are determined from this condition. Let us suppose a square redoubt. It is clear that
the distance between the crest and the terreplein being
4 yards (about), a square redoubt with faces equal to 8

yards, would have no terreplein, and could not therefore be occupied.

FIG. 67.

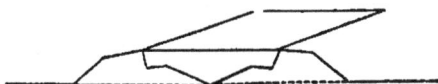

In increasing the dimensions of the faces, the surface of the terreplein increases rapidly, and the length of the face can be calculated so as to give sufficient surface for its garrison. In supposing one man per yard of parapet, and no reserve, it is found that the smallest square redoubt would have 58 ft. for side, and 77 men for garrison. But a work of this description is also impossible: the terreplein would be so crowded, that room would not even be left for the fall of a shell!

To obtain a work giving sufficient accommodation, it is necessary to count a reserve of one-third, and a minimum redoubt is obtained, fit for occupation. With two men per yard, or three, the minimum can be found.*

In making this calculation, when artillery is employed, it must be borne in mind that a gun takes 15 ft. of parapet, and requires from 400 to 600 square ft. of the terreplein. About 500 ft. are, besides, taken by the mask of earth (traverse), usually constructed in these en-closed works to mask the passage left for the en-

FIG. 68.

---

* See Appendix, Note III.

trance and egress of the garrison. By the same calculation, the minima of pentagonal or hexagonal redoubts
would be found.

As for Star Forts and Bastioned Forts, there is no need
of making such calculation for them, because there is always
more interior space enclosed than is required for the garrison.

(44) The minimum of such works is obtained from other
considerations. For star forts, the faces should not be less
than 30 yards, to avoid dead angles, which gives 360 yards
of parapet, for 6 salients, and 1080 garrison ; 480 yards for
8 salients, and 1440 men ; and for bastioned forts the length
of the smallest fronts has been shown to be equal to 200 yards.
The perimeter of a square fort with perpendicular $\frac{1}{8}$th, and
face $\frac{1}{3}$rd, is equal to 920 yards, and has a garrison of 2760
men.

(45) The force of a detachment being known, the perimeter
of an open work calculated on the base above mentioned, $\frac{1}{3}$rd
of the force ($\frac{2}{3}$rds for the banquette, $\frac{1}{3}$rd for the reserve), the
choice of the outline will depend upon the amount of labour
and the intrinsic value of the work. Thus, instead of a redan
having a development of parapet of 180 yards, and faces of

FIG. 69.

90 yards, a double redan would be better. In the same manner, instead of throwing up a redoubt of 360 yards perimeter, a star fort should be constructed, since its defence is better, and the amount of labour the same. Again, to a star fort of 920 yards' parapet, a bastioned fort should be preferred.

CHAPTER III.

DEFENCE OF FIELD-WORKS.

(46) The quality of a troop greatly enhances that of the fortification it is called to defend, yet the power of resistance of a work depends chiefly upon its outline. The ground, however, may in some instances so far influence the direction and length of faces, that the deficiency of the undefended space of salients and of the dead angles cannot be obviated by a sufficient amount of flanking fire. Several accessory means have therefore been had recourse to, in order to remedy these deficiencies, and complete the defence.

Sec. I. ARTILLERY.

(47) It is employed only in works likely to offer a good resistance, because the loss of guns is a serious check. It may be used to oppose the artillery of the enemy, to extend the action of the entrenchment to a further range, to flank a face or a ditch, to pour round or grape shot on the ground in front of the salients.

(48) When destined to flank or to fire in a constant direction, openings called *embrasures* are managed in the

parapet to fire through; when intended to command a surface of ground, and to fire in various directions, the guns are mounted on a mass of earth called a platform, and are said to fire "*en barbette*" (over the parapet).

A field gun fires at 8 ft. 6 in. above the ground; the surface of the *platform*, or its terreplein, is therefore at 3 ft. 6 in. below the crest, and the gun is carried there by means of a Ramp, 8 or 10 feet wide, and of a slope varying, according to circumstances, from $\frac{2}{4}$ to $\frac{15}{6}$.

A barbette is generally placed in capital, where it takes a circle of 12 feet radius.

Fig. 70.

Fig. 71.

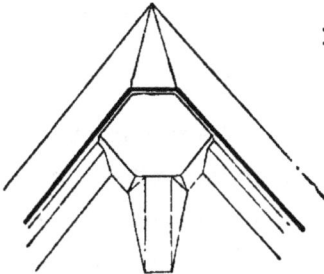

Along a face the platform is 15 feet wide and 24 feet long. Embrasures are "direct" (1) or "oblique" (2) when

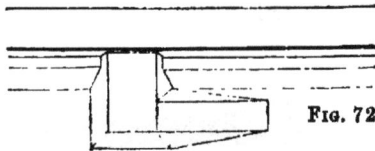

Fig. 72.

direct or oblique to the crest. They are 20 inches wide inside the work, and of a width equal to $\frac{1}{2}$ the parapet

Fig. 73.

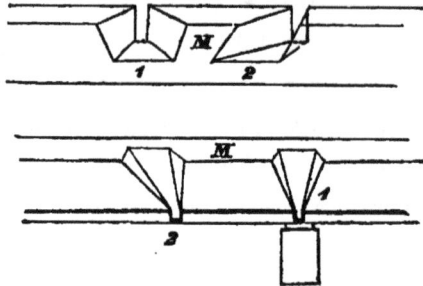

outside, their dimensions being measured on the *Sole* or bottom, the sides or *cheeks* slant at $\frac{1}{8}$ on the exterior slope, and are vertical on the interior. The sole slopes at $\frac{20}{1}$, the lowest part of the opening, or *genouillère,* is of course at 3 ft. 6in. above the ground.

(49) Both for guns firing en barbette and through embrasures it is advisable to place *platforms,* or floors of wood (9 feet by 15), to prevent the wheels from sinking into the earth; but when wood is not to be had, the earth is well

Fig. 74.

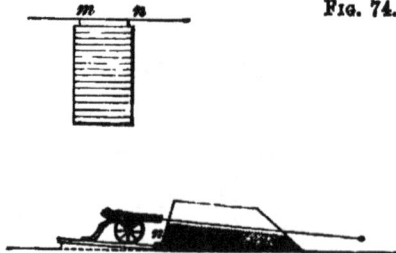

rammed in. A square piece of timber, *n, mn*, called a *Hurter*, prevents the wheels from touching, and therefore damaging the interior slope. These wooden platforms slope 6 inches from the rear to prevent the recoil.

(50) When a parapet is destined exclusively to cover a battery, the banquette is suppressed, and the *Epaulment*

Fig. 75.

thus formed has only three slopes—the interior at $\frac{2}{7}$ths, the superior at $\frac{10}{1}$, and the exterior at $\frac{1}{1}$. A height of $7\frac{1}{2}$ feet is sufficient.

In Permanent Fortifications the Platforms for the Barbette are often avoided, the gun being mounted on a carriage high enough to fire above the parapet.

Embrasures for guns should be pierced 18 feet apart, to leave room for the service of the guns, and the *Merlon, M*, or part of the parapet intervening between two adjacent embrasures, should never be narrower than 6 feet, to resist heavy metal (Fig. 73).

Sec. II. a. DEFENCE OF THE DITCH.

(51) To defend ditches where no flanking fire can be obtained, stockades, caponiers and counterscarp galleries

are employed; but wood must be at hand, and there must be time sufficient.

A *Stockade* is a strong loopholed Palisade, placed at the extremities of the faces of a redan, or at the shoulder angles of a Lunette, with means provided to get into the ditch.

Fig. 76.

(52) A *caponier* is a sort of block-house placed under the escarp of a redoubt; it communicates with the interior of the work by means of a gallery excavated under the parapet. The ditch must be enlarged in front of the caponier.

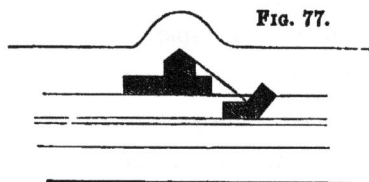

Fig. 77.

(53) A *gallery of the counterscarp* is a sort of caponier buried under the counterscarp at the salient of a redoubt, or any other work possessing unflanked ditches. The counterscarp in that case is not made circular, as is usually done at the salient angles, to diminish the déblai, but is kept parallel to the escarp. This sort of work has the

disadvantage of exposing its defenders to the liability of being cut off from the main force, in case the intrenchment fall into the hands of the enemy.

FIG. 78.

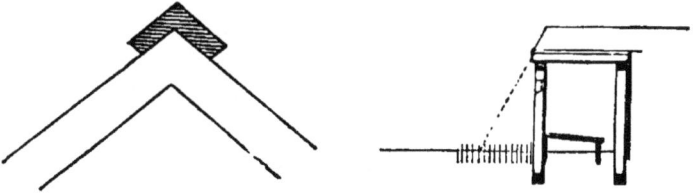

Caponiers and Stockades ought to be avoided when exposed to the enemy's artillery; the wider the ditch the greater is the danger, since a plunging fire can destroy

FIG. 79.

them at a long range. Counterscarp galleries offer in this respect a better disposition.

(54) When the faces of a work are of great length, it is found advantageous to break them, as represented in the

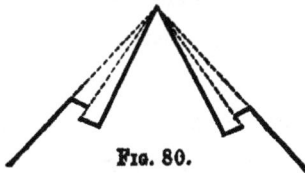

FIG. 80.

E

annexed diagram. This construction is called a *retirade*. The inconvenience of a dead angle no longer exists, since there is in MN sufficient space for a few men, who can fire on the enemy who would attempt to venture in the re-entering angle R of the ditch.

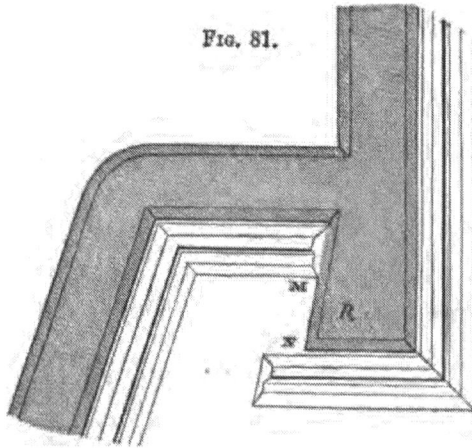

FIG. 81.

Sec. II. b. OBSTACLES.

(55) To hinder the approach of the enemy, to stop him under the fire of the intrenchments, to prevent his crowning the ditch, and to render the assault both a difficult and a murderous work, several accessory means (obstacles) are employed when the surrounding country offers the proper material, and when workmen are to be had. We shall successively pass these in review. Let it be premised that such obstacles cannot always be erected with regularity; an intelligent officer, when placed in a critical position, will at the moment of emergency turn to advantage the most

insignificant objects. It was thus that, in 1814, when the English surprised Berg-op-zoom, the division of Skerret repulsed from the town into one of the bastions, found there heaps of palisades freshly cut, and availing itself of this simple cover, it succeeded in checking the attacks of the French for a long time, and would have maintained its position had it not been turned by·the sailors, who scaled the escarp, whilst infantry renewed the attack in front.

The absence of obstructions in the unflanked ditches of fieldworks is a defect to be avoided *by all means.* At the siege of Toulon (1793) the great redoubt was carried by the French because their storming ·party, twice driven off, was permitted to re-form unmolested in the ditches. The redoubt of San Fernando, at Lerida (1810), was· in a similar case, &c.

(56) *Palisades* are·made of young trees, or larger ones split in two or three pieces, of a triangular shape, and pointed, 10 ft. long and 6 or 8 in. thick. They are placed 4 or 5 in. apart, and are buried 3 or 4 ft. in the ground,

Fig. 82.   Fig. 83.   Fig. 84.

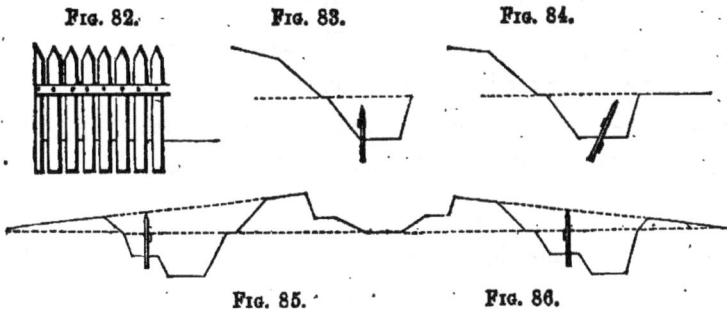

Fig. 85.   Fig. 86.

where they are fixed to a riband. Another riband placed on the inside, at 1 foot below the first, consolidates the structure. They are placed at the foot of the escarp, or of the counterscarp, and in the middle of the ditch; it is then better to incline them outside, it being more difficult for the assailant to cut them, but in no instance should they be exposed to artillery.

(57) *Fraises* are palisades placed horizontally at the crest of the escarp, or rather slightly slanting downwards; they must not project further than the foot of the escarp, in order not to afford cover. Two ribands, as is seen in the diagram, bind them together. A glacis usually connects them. They must also be placed on the counterscarp.

Fig. 87.

When placed on the escarp they offer a serious inconvenience. At the storming of Fort Picurina, at Badajos, in 1812, the assailants threw their ladders in the manner of bridges to the slanting stakes,—thus passed, and scaled the parapet by resting their ladders on the step formed by these fraises.

(58) *Stockades* are palisades touching each other, and loopholed for musketry; they may be called timber walls;

the timbers, 10 or 12 ft. long and about 9 in. square, are
sunk 2 ft. into the ground. The loopholes, cut between
two adjacent pieces, are 3 ft. apart, and 6 ft. above the
ground, with a banquette in the rear, or at 4 ft. only, with
a little ditch in front. They are employed, as is here seen,

Fig. 88.

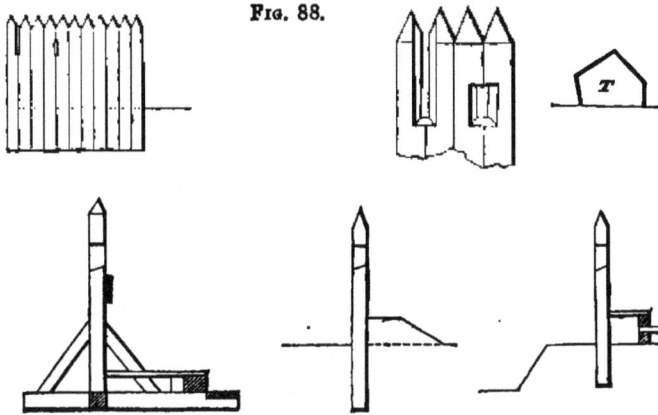

to flank ditches; when covering a gate or a communication,
T, they are called *Tambours*. They were first employed by
the Turks under the name of palankas. In the Burmese
war (1825) most of the enemy's works were mere stockades.

(59) *Abattis* are made with trees, or stout branches,
stripped of leaves and small branches, and sharpened; they
are intermingled, and their trunks well fixed in the ground
by a few pickets. Their usual place is before the counterscarp, where a glacis must defend them. This obstacle is
a very serious one, and we find numerous instances of its

FIG. 89.

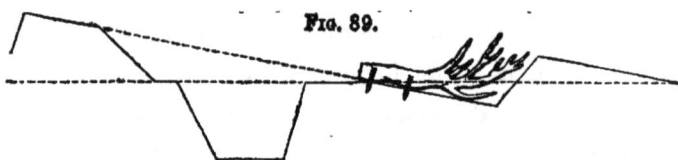

judicious selection,—at the battles of Fribourg (1644), of Malplaquet (1709), of Fontenoy (1745), &c. In 1792, the forest of Beval, between Weissenburg and Lauterburg, was rendered literally impenetrable by the French. In 1810, at Torres Vedras, the ravines were secured in that manner. At Sebastopol, in 1855, the Russians greatly increased the resistance of their works by means of abattis.

(60) *Chevaux de frise* are not so good, and require more labour; they are formed of a large joist, 10 or 12 ft. long and from 6 to 9 in. square, into the sides of which are driven wooden pins, 6 ft. long and 1 or 2 in. in diameter. Several are connected together by a chain. Sometimes

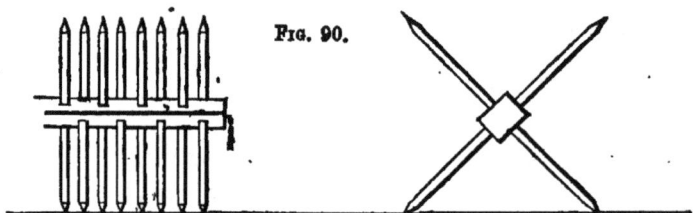

FIG. 90.

they are made of iron. They are chiefly employed to close the gorge of a work, to form barricades, and to arrest the inroad of cavalry.

(61) *Pickets*, from 1 to 2 in. in diameter, or thereabout, and from 2 to 3 ft. long, and pointed at both ends, afford a good obstacle when placed at small distances from one another. King Henry V. won the battle of Azincourt, in 1415, in consequence of having defended his bowmen with such pickets.

Fig. 91.

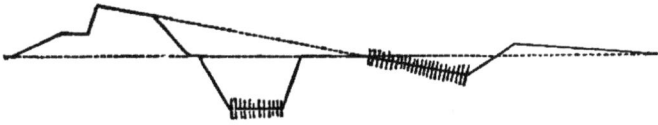

In the ditch before a caponier, or in front of the counterscarp, they may become a serious impediment.

(62) *Crows' feet* at the bottom of a ditch full of water, or under an inundation, are used like the pickets. They consist of stout nails 6 or 7 inches long, so connected that

Fig. 92.

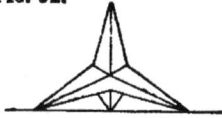

one point always stands upwards. When scattered on grass they are a serious hindrance to cavalry. The Romans, by the employment of crows' feet, were enabled to gain a complete victory over the Parthians, whose numerous cavalry would have overpowered the legions, greatly inferior in numbers. Bruce, at Bannockburn, is said to have employed them with advantage.

(63) *Military pits*, or *Trous de Loup*, placed in 2 or 3 rows in front of the counterscarp (at the salients, generally), are a formidable defence. Their depth may vary from 4 to 8 feet. A sharpened palisade is placed in the centre. The

Fig. 93.

Fig. 94.

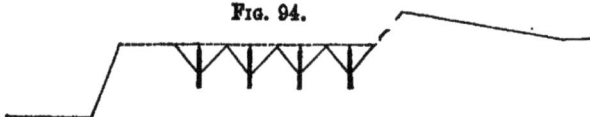

attack of the French on the Little Redan and the works on Careening Bay, in 1855, failed because the assailing columns were thrown into considerable confusion by rows of loop holes, into which the men stumbled in the midst of the darkness caused by dust and smoke.

(64) *Fougasses* are mines placed at the bottom of small shafts sunk in advance of the counterscarp. They are fired from the interior of the work, by means of a powder-hose brought along one side of the shaft, and carried through 6

Fig. 95.

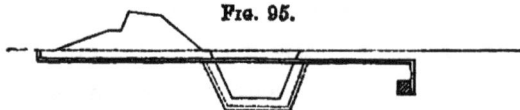

inches below the ground : the explosion breaks the ground, and throws the assailing columns into confusion. But they

are of difficult construction. Their distance to the counterscarp ought to be about twice their depth, otherwise the
explosion would destroy this scarp, the crater of explosion
being of a diameter equal to 1½ the depth.

Shell fougasses are formed of shells buried underground,
either singly or in rows : generally they are
placed in double boxes, the fuses passing into   FIG. 96.
a compartment full of powder, with which the
hose communicates. At Badajos the French
buried rows or chaplets of these shells along the counterscarp of the breached faces.

A *Stone Fougasse* is of easier execution. It consists of
an excavation 5 or 6 ft. deep, the axis of which makes an
angle of 45° with the horizon. The powder is placed at
the bottom of it, and covered with a strong shield of wood
at right angles to the axis, communicating with the work by

FIG. 97.

means of a hose. It is then filled up with stones, pebbles,
&c., and the upper part covered in with turf. A fougasse 6
yards wide and 5 deep, loaded with 50 lbs. of powder and
4 cubic yards of stones, when exploding scatters the material over a square of 55 yards wide. At Gibraltar (1782)
the defenders had recourse to them frequently.

Fougasses are sometimes formed under works for the purpose of destroying them when abandoned. In that case they must be laid 6 or 7 ft. below the centre of the parapet before the rampart is built. They may also be laid under the terreplein, as the Russians did at Sebastopol in their redans.

(65) *Inundations.*—When a stream is in the vicinity of a work, an inundation may be formed by constructing dams across the valley; the water thus swells above the banks and overflows the country. To be a serious obstacle, it should be deeper than 5 ft.; and when this depth cannot be attained, holes should be excavated here and there, and crows' feet employed, to render the access difficult.

The dams are generally constructed with a thickness of from 5 to 10 ft. at the top; the slope d'aval, $\frac{1}{1}$; that of à mont, $\frac{4}{1}$. Issues, or sluices, are disposed for the superfluous

Fig. 98.

waters. The dams must be protected by works or batteries in the rear.

Water may also be employed to fill the ditches of field-works; but this sort of defence fails in winter, and becomes dangerous; for when a garrison has to remain a long time in an inundated country, fever does more mischief than the enemy.

Sec. III. DEFENCE AND ATTACK OF FIELD-WORKS.

(66) Besides these means, any other that may be found on the spot can be turned to advantage. It is, indeed, of rare occurrence that a field-work can be defended by all these obstacles. An experienced officer will soon make the best of what he finds at hand. If nothing better can be obtained, he will collect stones in the interior to throw upon the assailants when they cross the ditch; scythes will serve his men to defend the superior slope, &c. The imperious necessity in which a commanding officer is placed to defend his work at all risks, will suggest to him what he has to do.

(67) If a village has to be put in a state of defence, besides the means above mentioned, others can be resorted to: barricading streets, loopholing walls and houses, converting hedges into breastworks, &c. The intrenchment for that purpose must be at some distance from the houses. If time fail, then an enclosure is made with the walls, hedges, houses, &c., that afford some flank defence, and tambours erected to complete it. All the houses, constructions, and trees on the approaches are levelled. If possible, a second enclosure is formed, then a third, so as to defend the ground inch by inch. A redoubt, usually the church, is fortified, loopholed, &c., to serve as a citadel or refuge to the defenders when the enclosure is forced.

The perusal of military history, and of campaigning, will here again form the judgment of the officer.

(68) All these works, defences, obstacles, &c., as we have previously said, will be of little avail unless the garrison is determined to fulfil its duty. "Fight to the last, regardless of danger!" ought to be the motto of all men called upon to occupy an intrenchment; "Devotion!" that of the commanding officer.

A strict and unremitting watchfulness will prevent surprises. Artillery will pour grapeshot on the columns of the assailants; musketry will tell on them when they become entangled in the obstacles; vigorous sorties will eventually repel the attack, if the latter have thrown their ranks into confusion; if not, bayonet and steel will resist the assault, and the defender mounted on the parapet will still fight at advantage. At last, when all is exhausted, and only then, retreat is thought of. Coolness and great decision are essential qualities in the officer; his example may decide the day; and, when commanding the evacuation, and, last of all, abandoning the intrenchment, he may say, that "all is lost, save honour!"

Field-works and fortified posts are not generally intended to make a defence of long duration; a day, or half a day, is considered a fair time; and it has often proved to be of an incalculable value. We have already mentioned the redoubt of Montenotte, which, for 24 hours, stood the repeated attacks of 12,000 Austrians, and thus gave the

victory to the French.   In 1793, the Dutch army was saved
by the resistance of the post of Werwick on the river Lys.
The same year the post of Turcoing defended itself a whole
day, and thereby prevented the French from attacking the
English.   The great redoubt of Fleurus (1794) saved the
French army from a defeat. Every one knows of the vigorous
resistance of the Austrian works at Jemmappes; of the Russian redoubts at Borodino ; of the hamlet of Hougoumont,
at Waterloo, &c.

(69) The attack of field-works is also an important consideration. It should always be preceded by reconnoitring.
Surprises sometimes succeed, but open force must be had
recourse to when good troops defend the intrenchment.
Artillery endeavours to destroy the obstacles at a distance;
then the columns of assault advance in several directions,
preceded by men carrying ladders, fascines, &c., to clear the
defences, and followed by reserves ; cavalry on the wings
are ready to repel sorties.   The assailants advance rapidly
to the counterscarp, and sappers and miners cut openings
through the palisades, stockades, &c.; then the assault takes
place.   In cases of repulse, artillery and cavalry protect the
retreat.

(70) In the interior of a large work it is sometimes found
advantageous to throw up a small intrenchment or redoubt
(réduit), overlooking the surrounding terreplein, either to
serve as a place of refuge to the garrison, and facilitate its

retreat, or to keep possession of the principal work with a small force. Such redoubts are difficult to establish in the field, inasmuch as they imply a work of great magnitude, and, unless the ground be very uneven, they would be too much exposed to the plunging fire of the enemy mounted on the parapets of the intrenchment. Besides, if the garrison perform its duty, it will remain on the banquettes to the last moment, and the enemy would enter into the redoubt pêle-mêle with the defenders. If, however, this interior redoubt be placed in some re-entering part, where the defenders can retire under the protection of its fire, it may become most useful. When a garrison, after having repulsed several assaults, has been reduced to a small number, and has become too weak to hope for a vigorous resistance, a redoubt can then serve as a refuge and a citadel.

A block-house may serve as a defensive barrack and interior trenchment, to guard a larger work. In mountainous countries, among hostile populations, such block-houses surrounded by field-works, which the garrison can defend if necessary, have been found most advantageous to occupy the chief passes, and to protect the resting-places of convoys.

(71) It is chiefly in the works destined to cover bridges (têtes-de-pont) that interior intrenchments are met with in the field. They are, in fact, indispensable. When the army retreats, it first collects behind the principal work, whose artillery and musketry delay the advance of the foe, and give time

to the troops to cross the bridges.   As soon as the principal
work has fulfilled that purpose, the redoubt continues to
keep the enemy in check in the terreplein in front, covering
the last retreating body ; and, as soon as the bridges have
been destroyed, its small garrison hastily retires in rafts or
boats kept ready for that purpose.   The tête-de-pont of
Cassel, constructed by the French in 1792, was intended to
allow space for 20,000 men to fight, and yet it could be defended by 3000 men only.   The works thrown up at Nord-
heim, on the Rhine, in 1744, by the Prince of Conti while
retreating, can be given as an example of the most judicious
employment of the têtes-de-pont with redoubts.   The têtes-
de-pont erected on the Vistula in 1806 and 1807, those on the
Danube in 1809, that at Dresden in 1813, that of Praga, on
the Vistula, at Varsovia, &c., present similar dispositions.

CHAPTER IV.

CONSTRUCTION OF WORKS.

(72) The outline and profile of a work having been selected, the construction of the intrenchment commences.

The line of fire is traced on the ground by means of a pickaxe, and strong pickets are planted at every angle.

To show the dimensions of the remblai, and guide the workmen, right profiles made with slips of deal are constructed along every face, some 10 yards apart. At the salient and re-entering angles oblique profiles are also erected, the position of their vertical poles being obtained

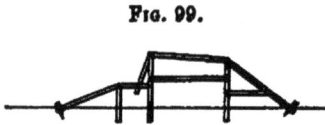

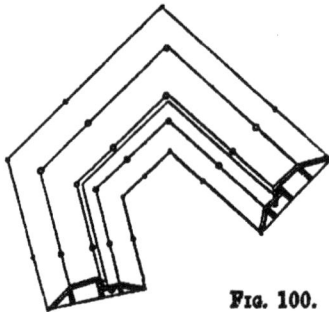

Fig. 99.

Fig. 100.

by the intersection of the lines passing through the corresponding poles in the contiguous faces; the slips marking the slopes, fixed and adjusted with those of the faces, so as to form regular plans.

(73) The ditch is not excavated at once, but by layers three feet deep; therefore, if the lines *AB* mark the proper

FIG. 101.

width of the ditch, the lines *CC,CC,* parallel to the crests of the scarps, are first traced with the pickaxe. When the excavation reaches 3 ft., then new lines are traced; when the depth averages 6 ft., new lines again show the déblai, the profiles of the déblai being as represented.

FIG. 102.

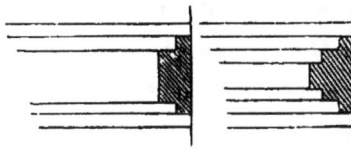

When the definitive depth is arrived at, the steps of the counterscarp are first cut away, then those of the escarp.

FIG. 103.

(74) The workmen are divided into small squads, occupying about five or six yards on the déblai, according to the nature of the soil and the depth at which they are

F

Fig. 104.

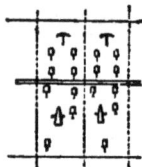

working, a greater number being necessary for a greater depth. Ten men form a good squad.

A pickaxe breaks the ground, two shovels next to him throw the earth towards the scarp, where two other shovels throw it up the berm; there again two shovels throw it on the profile. The remblai rises horizontally, one shovel equalizing the earth, and two men ramming it in. Fine earth should be reserved for the superior part of the parapet, to avoid splinters. The slopes steeper than ½ are supported by revetments, the others are pared when the work is completed. The terreplein, if necessary, is drained.

(75) The men composing a detachment are usually expected to throw up their intrenchments themselves; in some few instances, workmen are taken from among the inhabitants. It is then better to pay them by the task instead of by the day, and to fix the task and the price of labour. An officer will find it the best plan to employ at first a few men, and to pay them well for a day or two's work: it will soon regulate the daily task.

Field-works are often thrown up in a great hurry, and care must be taken not to begin a work unless there is a certainty of having it completed in due time. The following data will serve as a basis, supposing the number of men employed on the déblai to be the greatest possible:

A work of 8 ft. relief, with parapet 9 ft. thick, requires 8 days.
     „   7 ft.   „   7 ft.   „   6 „
     „   6½ ft.   „   6 ft.   „   4 „
     „   6 ft.   „   4 ft.   „   2 „

To obtain approximately the time required for a work of greater relief, multiply the thickness of the parapet by that of the relief; expressed in yards, the product gives the number of days. A work ten feet high, with a parapet twelve feet thick, will, then, require about $3\cdot3 \times 4 = 13\cdot2$, between thirteen and fourteen days. In urgent cases, this time may be reduced by half, by excavating on both sides.

FIG. 105.

.(76) If a work is to be thrown up in the proximity of the enemy when an attack may be made before it is completed, the parapet is no longer erected at once. It is at first made four or five feet thick, and in that state it is fit to resist musketry; it is afterwards widened, then raised to its proper height, the banquette and its slope being formed from earth taken from the terreplein. The work may thus be constantly kept in a defensive condition whilst being erected; but the ditch being rendered too weak, a glacis becomes necessary to widen or deepen it.

(77) *Revetments.*—The interior slopes, the cheeks of embrasures, the extreme profiles, and, in general, all the slopes of a steeper inclination than $\frac{1}{1}$, are supported by

revetments. These are made whilst the parapet is being constructed. The chief revetments employed in the field are *Sods*, or square pieces of turf cut from adjoining meadows and heaped one upon another; breaking the joints; secured to each other by pegs, to the parapet by brushwood.

Fig. 106.

(78) *Fascines* are a sort of fagot made of brushwood, firmly bound by several gads. Small fascines are 6 ft.

Fig. 107.

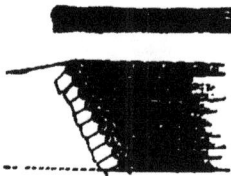

long and 7 in. in diameter. With stronger stuff, large fascines, 18 ft. long and 9 in. in diameter, are also made. They are secured to each other by pickets, and to the parapet by a picket in the middle. The joints must be broken, and at the angles the extremities should be alternately flush.

(79) *Gabions* are cylindrical ba kets, made of twigs, and

opened at both ends, 3 ft. high, and from 2 to 3 ft. in
diameter. They are in revetments placed close to each

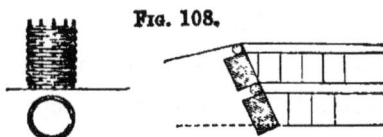

Fig. 108.

other, and two rows of fascines surmount the first row of
gabions.   Pickets strengthen the whole.   Fascines and
gabions are preferred for embrasures.

(80) *Hurdles* are formed by driving pickets 6 or 9 in.

Fig. 109.

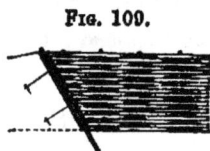

apart into the slope in the direction of the slope, and en-
twining twigs or rods with the pickets.

(81) *Sandbags*, made of strong canvas, are a poor
revetment, but are employed when no other can be had.
The bags are disposed as the sods, alternating headers and
stretchers, and breaking the joints. They are sometimes

Fig. 110.   Fig. 111.

placed three together on the parapet, to form a sort of loop-hole for the men to fire through. (Fig. 111.)

(82) *Planks*, when they are to be had, form a good revetment; casks, trunks of trees, &c., are all also employed.

It is not usual to give revetment to the scarps, except in works intended to stand for a long time; and where water is employed, then timber revetments are the best.

(83) *Communications.*—When an open work is com-pleted, its gorge is generally closed with palisades or *chevaux-de-frise*, with a barrier for the egress of the garrison. In enclosed works, an opening, two yards wide, is always left on the side the least exposed; and in order that the enemy may not see the defenders in reverse, a mass, called a *Traverse*, is erected inside, either with or without a banquette.

Fig. 112,

These traverses can be organized defensively by forming them of two parts respectively crossing their fire. In the

Fig. 113.

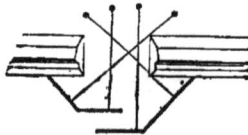

defence of a village, the above disposition has been found most advantageous. In 1757, when the Austrians found it impossible to batter down the walls of Gabel with their twelve-pounders, they forced open one of its gates, and some companies rushed into the town; but meeting with traverses in their front and on both flanks, they were obliged to retire with considerable loss.

We sometimes hear of cavalry storming field-works. This is a mistake. Cavalry cannot storm a work, but it may turn it, and when the gorge is not defended by palisades, barriers, &c., it can rush on the garrison, and become master of the intrenchment. At the battle of Borodino (1812), the French cavalry thus took the Russian redoubts. A similar occurrence had taken place in 1760, near Weissen-Hirsch, when the Austrians were marching to the relief of Dresden.

In Forts, the opening is left in the middle of the curtain,

Fig. 114.

and is covered by a small redan, or ravelin. It is either a mere palisade, itself provided with a barrier, or a regular redan, with its ditch communicating with that of the fort. In the latter case, a covered way is generally formed, and openings are formed in the face of the ravelin, and also in the covered way.

(84) To cross over the ditches of enclosed works, move-able bridges are formed; for narrow ditches, three or four sleepers laid across, and covered with plank, are sufficient. For a greater width, one, two, or three, or more trestles, support the sleepers.

FIG. 115.

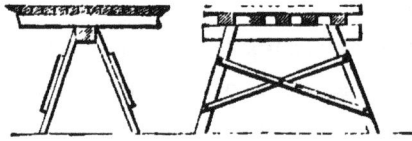

When the width is small, two little wheels adapted to the bridge permit it to be moved along the sleepers.

FIG. 116.

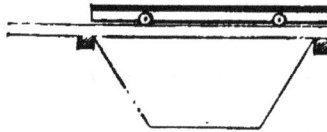

(85) *Defilade.*—When a field-work is to be erected in the vicinity of a height that commands it, nearer than the range of musketry, it becomes necessary to conceal its in-terior from the plunging fire of the enemy. This is done sometimes by modifying the outline (41); if not, we arrive at the solution of the question by altering the relief—an operation called *Defilade.*

This is a very important problem, inasmuch as the very purpose for which the fortification is made is not obtained if the men are not covered : they must move without being seen on the banquette and the terreplein.

In open works, the gorge is the limit to which the defilade must cover the garrison, and in lines, this limit must extend as far as 20 yards in rear of the innermost tracing, because much space is required for the large bodies generally occupying these works.

(86) Let us suppose a height H, within reach of musketry of a lunette, G a point of the gorge, and A the salient.

FIG. 117.

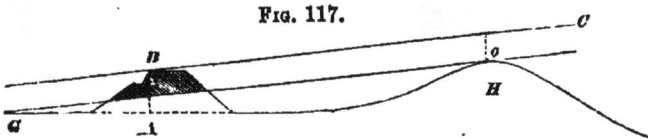

By the line of gorge and the commanding point O, we imagine a plan called the *Plane of Site*, whose tracing is here represented by line OG. Parallel to it, and at 8 ft. distance, another plane, whose tracing is here represented on BC, is called the *Plane of Defilade*.

If the crests of the work are kept in this plane, the terreplein and the gorge will evidently be covered.

The increase of relief must not exceed 4 ft., otherwise another position or another outline must be selected for the intrenchment.

The defilade can also be effected by sinking the terreplein and keeping it parallel to the plane of defilade.

Fig. 118.

In such case the ditch becomes smaller, or a glacis must be constructed to get rid of the surplus of earth. The first method is preferred in the field, when time is a matter of importance.

(87) This increase of relief answers the purpose when the height is in front of the work; but if it is on one side,

Fig. 119.   Fig. 120.

the face *AB* would be exposed to slanting and reverse fire, and a traverse or *Parados* must be constructed. Its crest is kept in the Plane of Defilade, passing through a line, at 6 ft. above the banquette.

Should the work be between two heights, a traverse may

Fig. 121.   Fig. 122.

 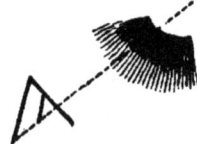

eventually protect both faces; but it is a most unfavourable case, and in many instances, especially with enclosed works, almost impracticable.

Advantage must always be taken of these traverses for the defences. The traverses for the defilade of Fort Little Gibraltar, at Toulon, were combined to contribute actively towards the defence, and the losses of the storming-party speak to their value.

(88) The Defilade, difficult to treat on paper, is most simple on the ground; it is done before profiling, by means of a triangle made of smooth lath from 8 to 4 ft. long.

At the angles of the work, poles are placed vertically. The officer lying on the ground at the gorge *AB*, or a few yards beyond, *CD*, places one side of the triangle on that line,

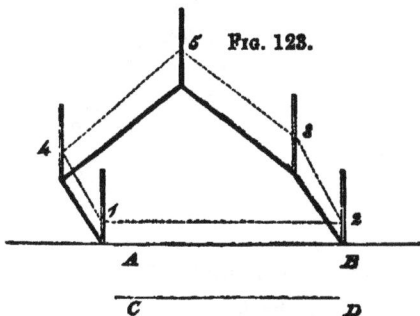

Fig. 123.

and causes its apex to ascend or descend until he finds the surface of the triangle tangent to the commanding point. The triangle in that position gives the plane of site, and the points 1, 2, 8, 4, &c., where its surface intersects the vertical poles are obtained immediately. By measuring 8 ft. above them, the relief required is found. Then the profiling begins. If, instead of the gorge, the limit of defilade must pass through a given point, as in the case of several commanding heights, then one of the angles of the triangle is placed on that point, and the triangle moved about it until its surface touches the points of command.

(89) When the ground only rises slightly in front of a salient, a mere increase of relief, 2 or 3 ft. on a length from 4 to 5 ft. of the parapet, called a *Bonnette*, is sufficient to

FIG. 124.

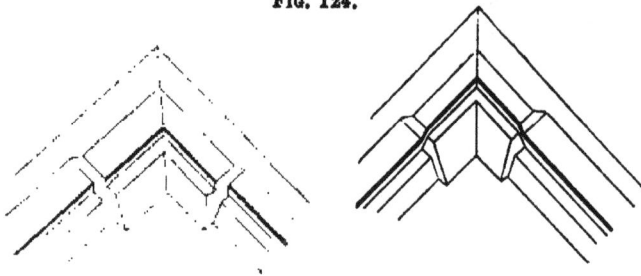

prevent the enfilade. They are sometimes employed along faces, between guns firing en barbette.

Traverses with fascine or gabion revetments fulfil the same purpose. Although these parados greatly increase the labour, and render the communication difficult, still, when time is abundant, they are most valuable. Passages are cut through them to enable the garrison to pass freely from one part to another, and they form a good shelter for powder magazines. Their profile varies: the thickness at

Fig. 125.

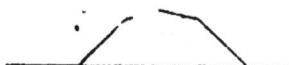

the top must resist artillery, from 6 to 9 feet. Its slope remains at $\frac{1}{2}$.

Chapter V.

Sec. I.   PERMANENT FORTIFICATION.

(90) Permanent Fortification has undoubtedly preceded field fortification, but its antiquity cannot be traced.   The first families that settled themselves in a village, or rather a collection of huts, protected them by palisades, formed of trunks of trees planted close together.   At a later period the use of stone became known, and towns were built. However, towns were a long time without being enclosed: plunder was the chief object of war, and cities becoming places of comparative safety, people retired therein during hostilities, with their riches.   Their population was scanty, and their surface contained a tract of ground sufficient to obtain by cultivation the necessary means of subsistence. The capitals of the states fulfilled that purpose, and they were the first fortified.   History teaches us that Uchoreus surrounded Memphis with parapets and ditches, with the double view of protecting the town against the Nile and the enemy.   In Assyria, Semiramis enclosed Babylon with walls; Saba, which Moses attacked, had also walls.   So long as the escalade was the only mode of attacking a town, a simple enclosure of walls was sufficient, but soon followed the machines which enabled men to approach these

walls under cover, to batter and overturn them. It was observed, that where the inequalities of the ground, or the form of the town, had given an irregular outline to these works, the enemy was sometimes exposed to view. The idea was taken and acted upon, and walls were constructed according to crooked lines in order to obtain a flank defence; this was afterwards improved by the addition of towers. The science of defence in ancient times does not

Fig. 126.

seem to have made rapid progress: all the science consisted in giving immense thickness (30 ft.) to the walls, piercing loopholes and machicoulis, giving great relief to the towers, and sometimes forming a double inclosure. This was the citadel, or place of refuge for the garrison when the enemy had succeeded in overthrowing the enceinte. The defence was based chiefly on the courage of the troops, the help of their machines, and the strength of the walls. Citadels were constructed on culminating points of the towns. The use of a ditch in front of an enclosure came later; it was originally destined to receive water.

(91) As long as the battering-ram was the only means of overthrowing the walls, fortification remained the same;

but when, in the middle of the fourteenth century, powder
gave to the besiegers a most prodigious power of percussion,
the rams were thrown aside, and artillery breached at a
distance even the thickest walls. To oppose this new mode
of attack, immense remblais of earth were accumulated
beyond the wall to increase the power of resistance, and to
furnish means for constructing an earthen parapet for the
defence of the breach. These remblais, or *Ramparts*, were
so called from the Italian, *parare*, protect; and the
syllabic iterative *ren or rem.*

(92) To obtain the earth for the rampart, as well as to
prevent the artillery from coming too near, the ditches
were widened and deepened, and counterscarps of masonry
erected.

The towers were abandoned as too small to receive a
parapet, and were replaced by *Bulwarks* (from the German
boll, empty, *werk*, work, probably because their centre had
an empty space left by the ramparts), works of the same
shape, but much larger. These were connected to the walls
by flanks destined to see or flank the foot of the escarp.

Fig. 127.

(93) It was soon found that the circular form could not answer, and it was replaced by two walls or faces directed towards or facing the country. This improvement is attri-

Fig. 128.

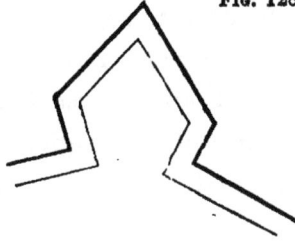

buted to the engineer of Verona, San Micheli (1523), and the use of these modified towers or *Bastions* has to this day been preserved.

From the time of San Micheli to this day, permanent fortification has been greatly modified, but the defence has not kept pace with the progress of the attack (*see* Chap. VI).

(94) When a town is to be fortified, we suppose it to be

Fig. 129.

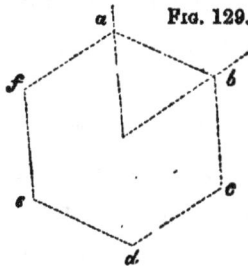

surrounded by an imaginary figure, *a, b, c, d, e, f*, called a *Polygon.* The sides *ab, bc*, &c., are called *Fronts.*

(95) When these fronts are of the same length, and the angles of the polygon equal, the fortification is called *Regular*. When, owing to the accidents of the ground, hills, rivers, &c., these fronts and angles are not equal and equidistant, the fortification is called *Irregular*.

The study of regular fortification forms the basis of the science; it is the province of the engineer to apply it to irregular sites in the best manner, a task sometimes eminently difficult.

The fronts being supposed to be equal in length, and exposed to the same dangers, it is evident that the combinations of their defence must be alike ; therefore the purpose of the study of Permanent Fortification is to find a perfect outline for one front—a problem still to be solved.

(96) The various lines constituting the trace or outline of a front, form what is called a *System of fortification*, and as every system results from a particular combination, it bears a particular name, usually that of its inventor.

The number of these Systems may be said to be indefinite, several hundred having successively been proposed, and many being still brought forward every day.

The outline of a system is independent of the length and disposition of the size of the fronts, and to facilitate the construction, rules or formulæ are laid down for every one of them.

To understand thoroughly the combinations adopted for the defence, it is necessary to be familiar with the method of attack, therefore we shall begin by giving the outline of a system (one of Vauban, for instance), and explain the process of attack, before proceeding any further in the modern improvements.

Sec. II.   VAUBAN'S FIRST SYSTEM.

(97) Vauban, a French general officer (1633–1707), is the author of several systems which bear his name. He never gave rules for their construction, but fortified towns as he found them, improving the fortifications already erected, and making the best of the sites. His name has become very popular, and in England he is generally considered as the inventor of the whole science. Such is not, however, the case; distinguished engineers had before him greatly improved the old outline of the clumsy bulwark, and his first system is but a slight modification, if even an improvement, on a system in use before his time.

He has done more against Fortification than for it; it is he who discovered the ricochet fire, and so much improved the means of attack, that the defence has ever since been unequal to it. His successors, in comparing the various fortresses he constructed, have for simplicity classified them into three systems. The second system is to be found only at Beford and Landau, and the third at New Brissach. To the first belong upwards of thirty places which he entirely constructed, and many more that he merely improved. This system we shall select for example (96), and explain it as required from Candidates for Military Service. But it must be borne in mind (and this we shall see hereafter), that Vauban had no fixed system at all, and that many modifications of the following method are to be found in his fortresses; still, as the formula adopted gives all the leading features of the first system, we select it.

(98) The line of front A B, is 360 yards; the perpendicular $= \frac{1}{8}$th of the front for the hexagon and all polygons

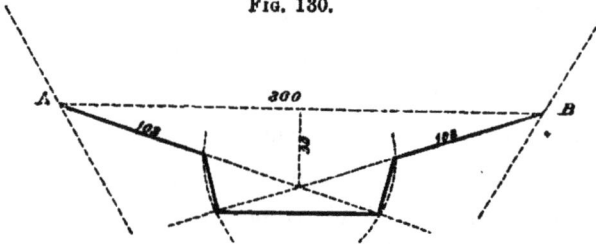

Fig. 130.

of a greater number of sides, $\frac{1}{7}$th for the pentagon, and $\frac{1}{8}$th for the square.

The faces $= \frac{2}{7}$ths of the front.

From the angles A, B, of the polygon as centres, and with a radius $=$ to the distance to the furthest shoulder angles, if arcs are described intersecting the lines of defence, the chords of these arcs give the flanks, and by joining their extremities the curtain is formed. (40.)

(99) The *main ditch* is obtained by describing from the salients as centres a circumference, with a radius of 30

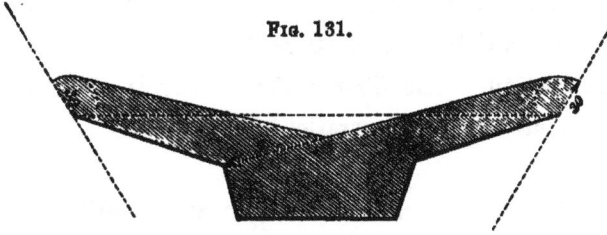

Fig. 131.

yards for a dry ditch, 36 for a wet one. Tangents to these arcs, drawn from the shoulder-angles, give the counterscarp.

(100) The *Tenaille*, in the Main Ditch, coincides with the Line of Defence; its thickness is 16 yards. Its ex-

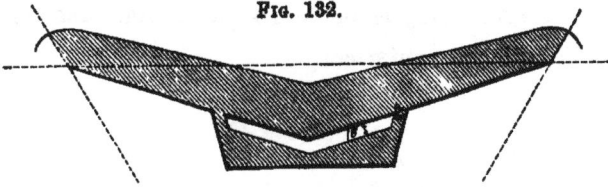

Fig. 132.

tremities are parallel to the flanks of the Bastions, and 8 yards from them.

(101) The salient of the *ravelin* is on the perpendicular

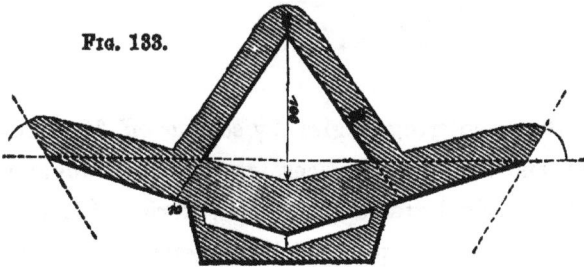

Fig. 133.

at 100 yards from the re-entering angle of the counterscarp.
Its faces are directed to a point 10 yards from the shoulder-
angle of the bastion. The ditch of the Ravelin is 20 yards
wide, and its counterscarp is parallel to its faces.

(102) In the main ditch, and between the tenaille and
ravelin, a double *caponier* is usually placed; its crests are
parallel to the perpendicular, and at 6 yards from it; the
foot of its glacis parallel to its crests at 20 yards. A passage
of 3 yards is reserved between the head of the caponier and
the ravelin.

(103) The *Covered way* is made 10 yards wide, and its
crest is parallel to the counterscarp.

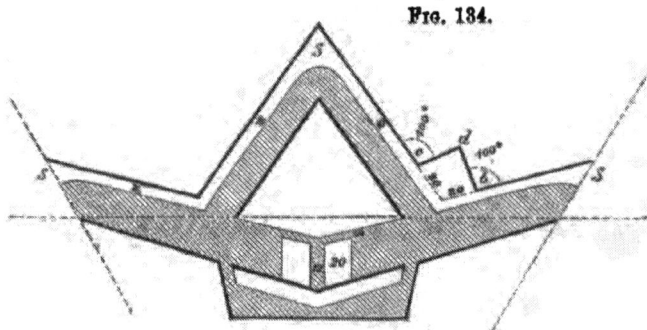

Fig. 134.

(104) At the re-entering angles, by setting off 30 yards
on each side, and drawing the faces, *db, dc*, at an angle of
100° with the original tracing, the *Re-entering Place of
Arms* is found. The terreplein of the covered way, at the

salients, *S, S, S*, forms the *salient places of arms*. The foot of the glacis is parallel to the crest of the covered way, and at 50 yards.

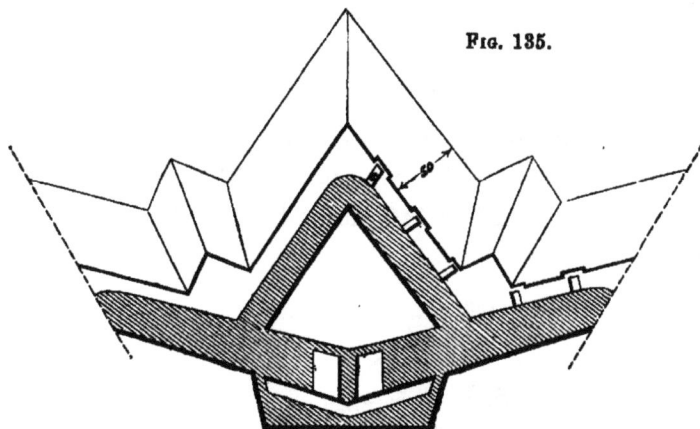

Fig. 135.

(105) *Traverses* are constructed in the covered way; they are 18 ft. in thickness. Those that enclose the Salient Places of Arms are formed on the prolongation of the faces of the Ravelin and Bastion. At the Re-entering Places of Arms they are perpendicular to the counterscarp. Midway in the branches of the covered way of the ravelin is another traverse, also perpendicular to the counterscarp.

(106) The first line of Parapet that encloses the place, consisting of Bastions, Flanks, and Curtains, constitutes what is called the *Body* of the Place, or *Enceinte*. Within the glacis, works like the Tenaille, Caponier, Ravelin, Covered Way, &c., are called *Outworks*. Any work erected

beyond the glacis, and within musketry range, is denomi-, nated an *Advanced Work*, to distinguish it from *Detached Works*, which are beyond range, although connected with the general defence of the place.

(107) The following cuts contain the *profiles* of the various parts of this front; the line *A B* represents the level of the ground in Figures 136, 137, 138, and 139; *a b* the level of the covered way in Fig. 140, and *c d* that of the main ditch in Fig. 141.

Fig. 136.

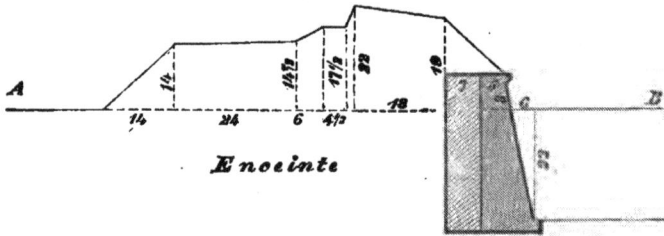

Enceinte

Fig. 137.

Ravelin.

FIG. 138.

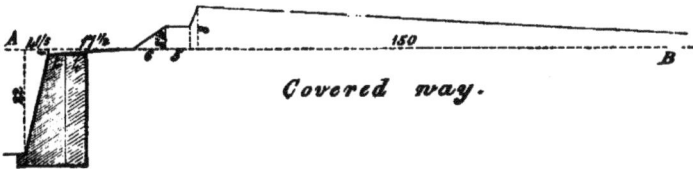

Covered way.

FIG. 139.

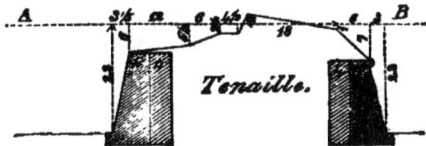

Tenaille.

FIG. 140.

Traverse.

FIG. 141.

Caponier.

(108) The rampart follows the outline of the crest of the bastion, having in its centre an interior space on the level of the ground,—the bastion is then called *Empty* or *Hollow.* If the interior is filled up to the level of the terreplein of the rampart, the bastion is called *Full.*

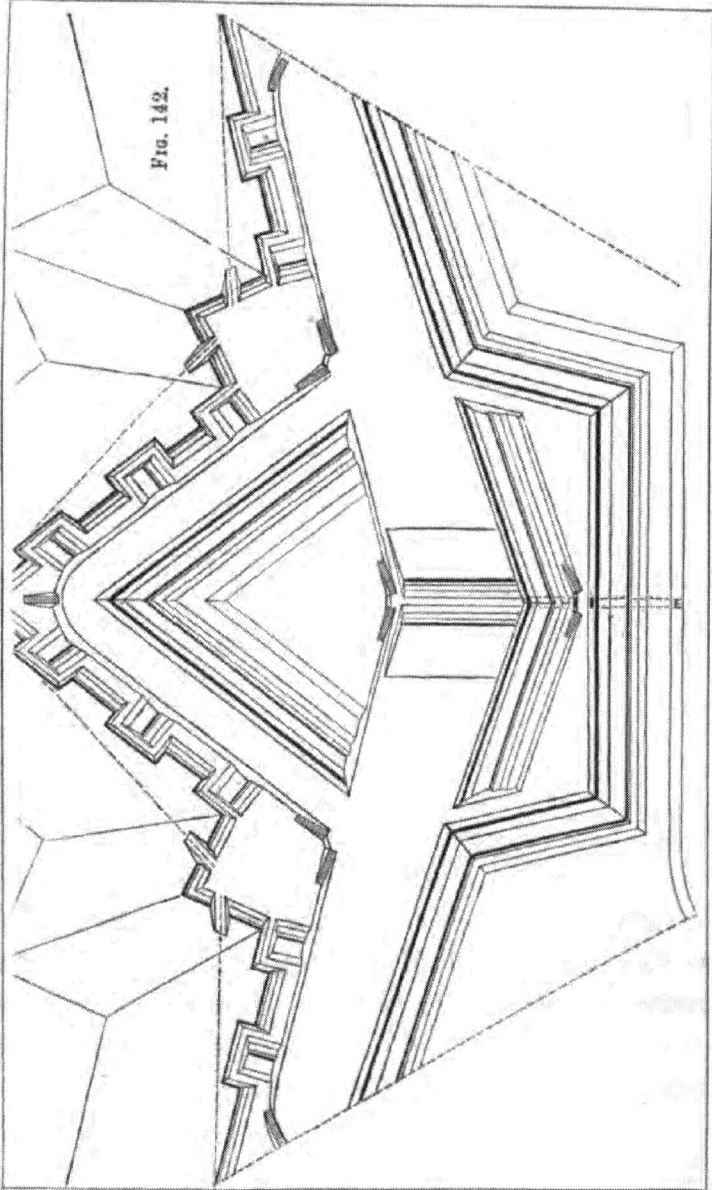

Fig. 142.

(109) Staircases, called *Pas de Souris*, 6 ft. wide, give access from the ditch to the Tenaille, Ravelin, Re-entering

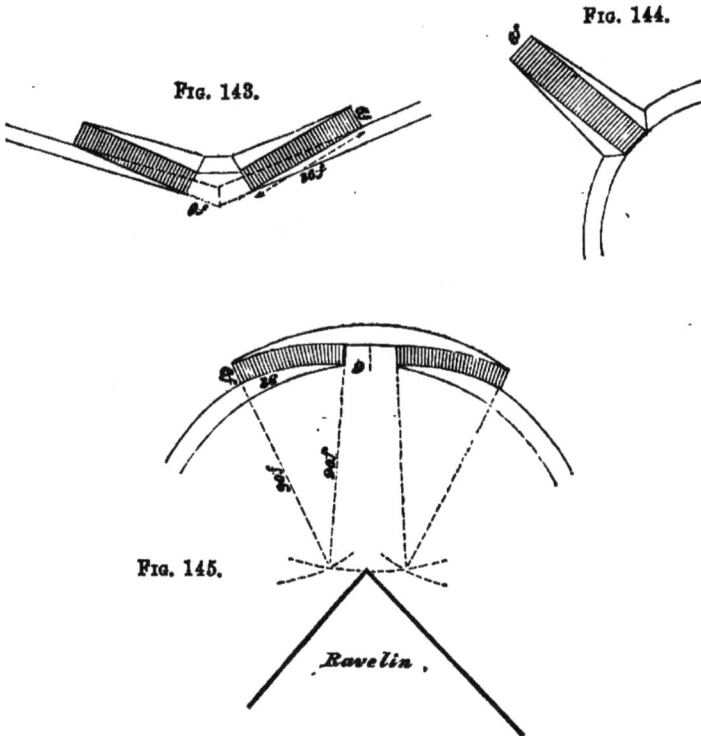

FIG. 144.

FIG. 143.

FIG. 145.

Ravelin,

and Salient Places of Arms; they are 36 ft. long, except for the Tenaille, where they are only 30 ft.; they are constructed at the gorge of the works, and are usually double.

(110) In the covered way, passages, 9 ft. in the clear, called *Crochets*, are managed around the head of every traverse.

(111) The covered way communicates with the country by *Sally Ports* or cuttings, 4 yards wide, 8 yards long, made in the glacis, in the middle of every face of the Re-entering Place of Arms. To mask them from the view of the enemy, they are directed towards the adjacent salients of the covered way. (*See* Fig. 136.)

(112) The communication between the place and its out-

Fig. 146.

Fig. 147.

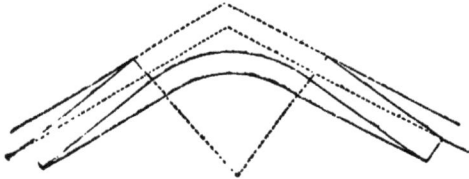

Fig. 148.

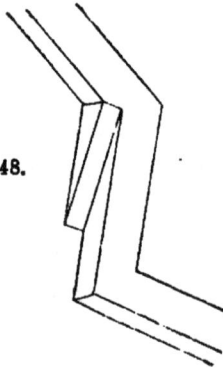

works takes place through a *Postern*, or gallery, under the curtain opening at the foot of its escarp.

Along the ramparts, Ramps, from 4 to 6 yards wide and 20 to 30 yards long, are constructed to facilitate the passage of men and artillery. The Figures 147, 146, 148, represent these ramps at the salient of the ravelin, on the curtain, and on the flank of a bastion.

(113) To separate wet ditches from dry ones, a wall, called a *Batardeau* is built across; and to prevent it from serving as a passage, it forms an angle at the top, and a tower of solid masonry is erected on its middle. In these

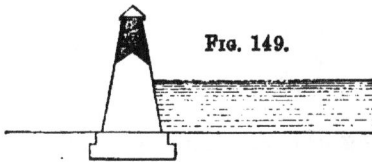

FIG. 149.

batardeaux sluices are usually placed, in order to fill up the dry ditch, if necessary, when the besieger attempts to carry his approaches there. Batardeaux are generally constructed at the salients of Bastions.

(114) Vauban has given to the revetments of the scarps a slope of $\frac{1}{5}$ for all heights, thereby obtaining massive walls for low scarps, and weak ones for high relief. These walls, 4 or 5 ft. thick at the top, are strengthened by buttresses, or *counterforts*, on the rear, some 15 ft. apart, whose effect

is to relieve the wall, and to resist the breaching batteries
more readily than a plain scarp of superior thickness. The
foundations are 3 ft. deep, and their breadth exceeds by
18 in. that of the revetment. At the top of the escarp a
coping-stone, *A*, projects, to prevent water from running
along the slope and filtering through the joints. It forms

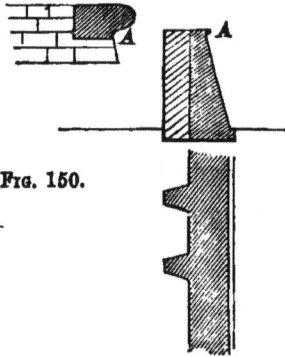

Fig. 150.

a continuous *cordon* all along the magistral line of the
enceinte and of the ravelin.

(115) Such is the first System of Vauban. To understand its value it is necessary to know the method of attack
to which it must offer resistance, and this we shall examine
in the next Chapter. Though the chief reliance is placed
on musketry in the defence, it is none the less a fact that
Artillery is the essential element in the defence of a fortress.
Bousmard calls it the soul of a place; Carnot says that a
fortress is but an immense battery, &c. To the garrisoning
and armament of fortresses, we shall direct our attention;

of course the guns are employed chiefly on the front attacked,—some flanking the main ditch, some that of the ravelin; others on the capitals of the bastion or ravelin commanding the approaches, and on the faces of the latter a few guns flank the salients of the bastion.

Chapter VI.

ATTACK AND DEFENCE OF A FORTRESS.

Sec. I. IRREGULAR ATTACKS.

(116) Permanent Fortification, we repeat, cannot be learnt unless the attacks be thoroughly understood. We shall therefore dwell on this subject, and at the same time that we explain the method adopted for the attack we shall give the conduct of the defence, both being so intimately connected that any attempt to study them separately could but bring confusion.

The hostile efforts directed against a fortress are of two different sorts: to the first category belong all those that are not regulated by fixed rules, to the second those that are conducted according to rules given by experience, the *ensemble* of which constitutes the art of sieges.

(117) In the first place is the *surprise*, but this is now of very rare occurrence. Its success depends on intelligence with the interior of the place, and the manner in which the service is performed; it is usually combined with *attacks of Vive Force*. But the garrison must be weak, and the scarps easy of access. Secrecy and rapidity of

execution are most essential, since, in case of failure, the retreat must be made under the fire of the place. Besides, the forces must be considerable, for the garrison may rally to a central point, and then charging the scattered columns of the assailants, easily overpower them. Prague, garrisoned with 2000 regular troops and 3000 irregular, was surprised by the French in 1741. Schweidnitz, with 8000, was taken in the same manner by General Laudun in 1761. Owing to a door badly constructed, through which the French musketeers found an entrance, Valenciennes was taken in 1667. Great danger however attends these operations, and although the Crimean army has been found fault with for not attempting to take Sebastopol by a *coup-de-main*, yet it acted according to the rules of experience. At Cremona, in 1702, Prince Eugene contrived to enter by night with 4000 men, and to carry off the Governor, Marshal Villeroy, but an Irish regiment eventually drove him away. At Berg-op-zoom, in 1814, the English had already surprised and occupied several bastions, yet they were repulsed with considerable loss. It is important to know the disposition of the works, the depth of the ditches, and the height of the scarps; to provide the men with ladders of proper length; to be aware of the negligences habitual in the service, &c. The attacks should never be attempted at night; the scarps of the Ravelin being often mistaken for those of the enceinte, the columns lose their way, and the confusion becomes great.

Early in the morning is the best moment; the columns

H

of attack must be strong and well supported; the commanding officer should be a man of action, well acquainted with what he has to do when once in the place, or when he has to retreat. These attacks are only made now when a powerful reason, such as the arrival of hostile reinforcements, compels the general to make a desperate effort before retiring.

(118) *Bombardment* has generally but little effect, since both the men and ammunition in a garrison are usually provided with bomb-proof shelters; the strength of the fortress is not much impaired, the houses only suffering much.

With populous towns, little disposed to resist, it may answer; but if the garrison is determined, shelter will soon be constructed and fires extinguished. These attacks are of difficult execution, and require enormous power of transport.

(119) *Blockades* are resorted to against a garrison numerous but badly provisioned—an occurrence more frequent than is generally supposed. In 1806, after the battle of Jena, the French found large bodies of Prussian troops heaped, so to speak, in fortresses. In that case it is essentially necessary to blockade exactly all the circumference, and to occupy vigorously all the strong points, in order to suppress any attempt on the part of the enemy to evacuate.

(120) *Siege.*—Regular attacks proceed more slowly, but are more certain; to take up a position around the place, intercept all communication with the exterior, approach nearer and nearer up to the crest of the glacis, open a breach in the enceinte, reach the garrison, and compel it to surrender,—such is their ensemble.

These attacks once begun must be carried on without interruption, otherwise the garrison will construct new intrenchments, replace its parapets, and organize a more powerful defence; they should therefore only be undertaken when there is a certainty of the arrival of tools, artillery, ammunition, &c.

This question of tools and implements is very important, and although their quantity varies with the strength of the place and that of its garrison, yet an idea may be formed by observing that the most recent sieges give, as necessary, an average of 7000 pickaxes, 10,000 shovels, 3000 axes, 5000 hatchets, besides special tools for sappers and miners. The implements required are 7000 fascines for trenches, 100,000 ditto for revetments, 20,000 gabions, 10,000 fagots for sapping, 50,000* sandbags, besides a proportional number of pickets, hurdles, sap rollers, blinds, &c.

---

* At the siege of Gerona (1809), by the French, one battery of 16-pounders alone required 80,000 sandbags.

At Constantine, in 1837, the number of sandbags employed in the construction of the batteries was enormous.

Sec. II.　SIEGE.

(121) The first operation made by a besieging army is the *Investment* of the place.

Its object is to cut off all communication with adjoining towns or corps of troops, to prevent the garrison from getting rid of encumbrances, to lay hands upon all neighbouring and distant resources, such as corn, cattle, wood, &c., to intercept any detachment not actually in the place, and to favour the reconnoitring—an important item, which will spare false movements and loss of time.　To insure success, the investment should be sudden.　It is generally carried out by detachments of cavalry and field-artillery, which during the day keep themselves out of range, and approach nearer at night.　Their strength varies with local circumstances, and their march is regulated so as to bring them at the same time before the place.

(122) The army follows one or two days after.　In the mean time, the position of the camps has been determined by reconnoitring; they are usually out of range (three thousand yards from the glacis), and the best use is made of the ground.　Sometimes barracks are constructed.　The parks of artillery destined to receive the ordnance stores and ammunition, and the engineers' park for the tools and implements, &c., are formed at the same distance.

(123) Whilst the troops are encamping, field-works are thrown up to occupy the chief points and protect the parks and magazines of all sorts against surprise; and such bridges, trenches, &c., as are necessary to connect the investment, are constructed. In early times it was customary for the besieger to intrench himself between lines of circumvallation and contravallation, the former to resist the sorties, the latter to protect the rear against any attempt made to force him to raise the siege. This method is now obsolete. The lines of circumvallation are to a certain extent replaced by the trenches themselves, and a few redoubts on the flanks. As for the lines of contravallation, experience has proved that they are dangerous (39) as defensive positions, unless the enemy can present himself on a limited front only. It is better, in case of an attack on the rear, to leave sufficient forces to guard the trenches, and to march to the enemy.

(124) In the meanwhile, officers proceed to make an accurate reconnoitring of the place, in order to determine the point of attack. During the day, they advance with a small escort to within 400 or 500 yards of the glacis. At night they endeavour to reach the covered way, fathom the depth of the ditches, &c. Plans of most fortresses are always to be had: the reconnoitring then completes the information. In the selection of the point of attack, the nature of the soil has a great influence, a rocky soil being

an insurmountable obstacle. Marshy and gravelly soils are to be avoided, as well as those which are liable to be inundated. A river is also a serious obstacle.

The configuration of the ground is next considered. When it rises towards the place, it facilitates the defilade, but is very disadvantageous for the batteries; hollows running perpendicularly to the front are dangerous, but a ridge affords good support to the trenches, and may eventually mask them.

It is important to direct the attacks upon points where a superiority of fire can be obtained; therefore re-entering angles and straight lines are left, and salients are selected. These are examined, as well as the works that support them; their flank defences, the height of their escarps, their dry or wet ditches, the number of outworks to be successively carried, the facilities for the besieger to throw up intrenchments on these points, &c. The proximity of woods, the facility of communication, the line of retreat, &c., all these influence the selection of the attack.

(125) The point of attack being selected, the commanding officer of engineers draws the project of attack, assisted by the officer commanding the artillery; and the commander of the forces decides, in case any difference of opinion should arise.

This project generally embraces one front only, and consists of three partial attacks, one on the ravelin, one on each bastion. Attacks on two fronts require a very large force, and if the two fronts are not contiguous, they demand a double army.

When the angle of the polygon is very obtuse, it is better to attack two ravelins and a bastion, otherwise the collateral ravelins *AA* would become a serious impediment, their fire taking the attacks in flank.

FIG. 151.

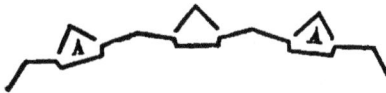

If the angle of the polygon is less, it is better to select two bastions and their ravelin; the collateral works give but an oblique defence, and the besieger has the advantage of giving two simultaneous assaults on the body of the place.

FIG. 152.

(126) *First Parallel.*—Let us suppose that the attack is made on a Ravelin and two Bastions. The first step is to throw up a continuous intrenchment that will serve as a basis to the subsequent operations. It is parallel to the general contour of the fortress: hence its name of Parallel. It is constructed at 600 yards from the most advanced salient of the place, because at that distance the troops employed to break the ground are not much exposed to grapeshot; the garrison cannot hear the noise, and is too

far off to attempt a sortie; besides, experience shows that at this distance, three-fifths of the rounds fired from the batteries established before the parallel take effect; at a greater distance the practice would become too uncertain. Sometimes an accident of the ground permits the parallel to be established at a smaller distance.

In 1794, at the siege of Maestricht, a hollow within a small distance of the place served to establish the extremity of the parallel. At Bouchain, a hollow within twice pistol-range allowed the besiegers to construct a place of arms (133) the first night of the opening of the trenches. At Limburg, the dragoons succeeded in forming a lodgment (143) within pistol-range, under cover of some hedges. At Bayonne, in 1814, a hollow road parallel to the works enabled Wellington to come within 240 yards of the place. At Malta, in 1800, fences of stone were similarly turned to account by the besiegers.

The tracing of the parallels, due to Vauban,* is very important: they must extend on both sides, to embrace all the works that have views on the attacks. Their outlines give to the besieger an immense advantage, to repel the sorties, to flank the zig-zags, to protect the batteries, and to connect all the attacks. The First Parallel is traced on the ground by means of pickets close enough to guide the engineers during the night. At the same time that it is being traced,

---

* He employed them for the first time at the siege of Maestricht, in 1673.

the direction of the capitals, as well as the alignement of
the faces of the ravelins and bastions, which must have

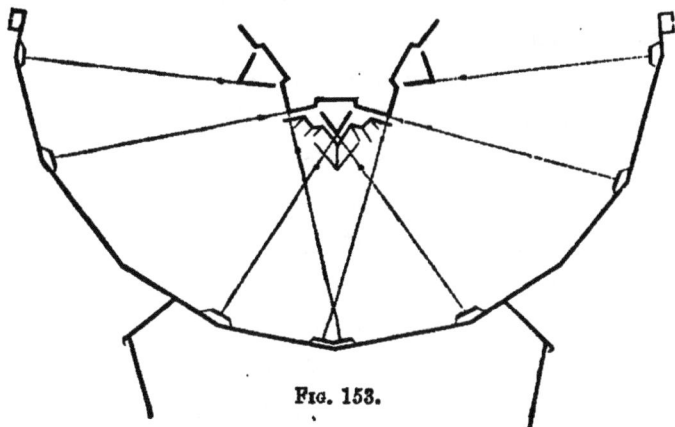

Fig. 153.

been accurately determined, are marked on the ground by
pickets. This operation is of the utmost importance, but
difficult in practice, since the glacis and outworks conceal
the escarps from the besieger; still it is to be done by
observing the exterior slopes of the parapets at sunset and
sunrise (when the difference of shade is of great help), by
mounting on ladders, &c.

Between the first parallel and the parks, at 1200 or
1500 yards from the town, *Entrepôts* are thrown up to
facilitate the communication with the trenches. They are
connected with the first parallel by zig-zags.

(127) When the tracing of the parallel is completed, the
number of workmen necessary for its execution is easily

calculated. At nightfall these workmen, carrying their muskets slung, are collected in the *entrepôts*, where they receive a shovel, a pickaxe, and a fascine each, and are formed into as many detachments as there are capitals crossing the parallel. It is important to deceive the garrison as to the time fixed for the "*opening of the trenches*," therefore it is only at night that this detachment, commanded by its officers and guided by engineers, marches to the tracing of the parallel, filing off right and left as they arrive there, and lying flat on the ground. Every man places his fascine before him, the engineers ascertaining that they follow the outline exactly. At a signal the men begin to excavate, throwing the earth before them to form a cover.

These workmen are protected by a guard calculated at three-fourths the strength of the garrison : the cavalry are at the extremities of the parallel, ready to charge; the infantry, twice as numerous as that of the enemy, takes up a position in rear of the workmen; wherever favourable accidents of ground occur, it sends battalions 20 yards in front, which detach picquets; these vedettes, &c., besides frequent patrols.

(128) During the first night the parallel is excavated 5 ft. wide and 3 ft. deep, and the communications with the

FIG. 154.

entrepôts are also executed with the same profile. Next day, both workmen and guard are relieved, and the trench is widened to 10 ft., slanting in the rear to carry off the water and defilade the space, the guard taking position in the parallel itself.

FIG. 155.

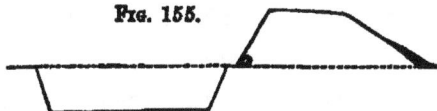

To enable the guard of the trenches to fire over the parapet, two steps, supported by fascines, are constructed

FIG. 156.

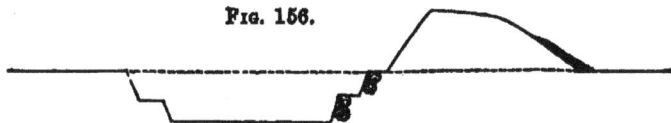

in the space between the capitals, and in some part of the parallel similar steps are cut on both sides of the parapet,

FIG. 157.

to permit the troops to clear the parallel easily, in order to march against the sorties of the besieged.

(129) *Batteries.*—When the first parallel is completed, batteries of enfilade and ricochet are raised on the spot where the prolongations of the faces of various works inter-

sect the parallel : those for direct and vertical fire are constructed opposite to the faces to be counter-battered. The object of these batteries is to subdue the fire of the defence, to permit the further advance upon the place. They are constructed by troops of artillery, and must be ready to open their fire in thirty-six hours after their tracing. The figures 158 and 162 show their situation.

The erection of these batteries varies with the accidents and nature of the ground. They are distinguished as—

Cavalier Batteries, when the platform of the gun is above the ground.

Fig. 158.

Elevated Batteries, when the platform is on the ground.

Fig. 159.

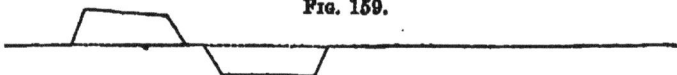

Sunken Batteries, when the level of the platform is below the ground.

Fig. 160.

Half-sunken, when the earth for the parapet is excavated both from the front and the rear.

Fɪɢ. 161.

The two latter are the most frequently employed.

(130) Trenches are then pushed onward in the shape of *zig-zags ;* they follow the capital because they thus occupy the undefended space before the salient, and do not obstruct the batteries of ricochet. These zig-zags must pass at 30 yards before the most advanced salients, and their tracing is contained between two lines, from 20—25 yards distant at the front, 35—40 in the rear ; in this manner they are defiladed and well flanked by the parallel. A return of 20 ft. is made at every extremity : they are executed on the second and third night.

(131) *Second Parallel.*—On the 4th night, the second parallel is executed at 275 or 300 yards from the salients

Fɪɢ. 162.

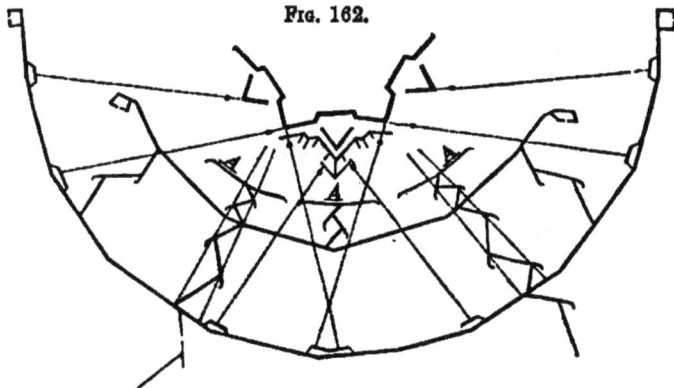

(Fig. 162). As it is nearer range, it must be constructed with greater care. The engineers trace it on the third or fourth night; next evening, the workmen collected in the depôts are marched down as for the opening of the trenches, carrying two light gabions (2 ft. 9 in. wide, 3 ft. high), a spade, and a pickaxe each.

Arrived on the spot, they place their two gabions 2 ft. beyond the tracing, and lie flat on the ground till the signal for the excavation to begin on all the line. The gabions are filled up in 15 minutes, and afford a musket-proof shelter. This process is called the *Flying Sap.* The first night the excavation is made 5 ft. wide, and the next day is enlarged to 10 ft.

Fɪɢ. 163.

Fɪɢ. 164.

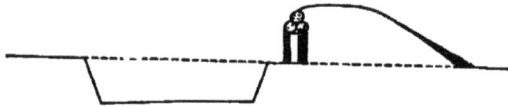

Banquettes are also erected for the guard of the trenches, and steps for passing over.

Fɪɢ. 165.

Fig. 166.

As is seen by these profiles, the second Parallel has a greater solidity, being provided with a revetment, to resist the projectiles.

This parallel is protected in flank by redoubts, or is connected to the first by zig-zags. When the ground masks the batteries, new ones must be constructed on the corresponding points of the second parallel: this is usually done in the 5th or 6th night. Their fire must be unremitting.

(132) In the meanwhile, the garrison do not remain inactive. As soon as the town is threatened with an attack, all the ditches in front of the place are filled, and the houses, walls, hedges, trees, &c., and all the agricultural buildings, levelled. Sometimes suburbs are intrenched, when they are likely to check the advance of the enemy.

The banquettes and interior slopes, ramps, &c., are repaired, platforms for guns are constructed, palisades are placed all along the banquette of the covered way, and the passages of traverses and sallyports shut with barriers: if possible, a second row of palisades is planted in the terreplein of the covered way.

At the same time tools and implements are collected, at the rate, for 1000 men, of 100 axes, 200 hatchets, 150 wheelbarrows; 10,000 sandbags, 200 chevaux-de-frise, &c.; wood is stored for stockades, galleries, mines, &c. At least 500 gabions, 2000 fascines, 600 hurdles, &c., are prepared for revetments.

Bomb-proof shelters are constructed for the troops, magazines, cisterns, &c. The artillery is placed on the ramparts.

After the investment, patrols reconnoitre to ascertain the day appointed for the opening of the trenches; redans, or *Flêches*, of 40 yards face, are rapidly thrown up in capital at the front of the glacis, to hinder the approach of the besieger. Lines of *Counter-approach*, a sort of trench, are excavated in front of the glacis, to be connected with batteries hastily thrown up on positions where the zig-zags can be enfiladed.

The establishment of the Russian rifle-pits, and the erection of their works on the Mamelon, in February, 1855, are instances of what a determined garrison can do to impede the progress of the besiegers.

All the artillery that can be spared is brought to the front of attack. Sorties at the opening of the first parallel are rather dangerous. Traverses and parados are raised to resist the ricochet batteries. While the second parallel is constructing, sorties, well supported by cavalry, become more easy; still they require prudence. Vauban said, that the loss of one man of the garrison is equal to that of seven to the besiegers. Sorties are usually made at night.

Sec. III. SIEGE.

133) *Demi-Parallels.*—From the second parallel the besieger advances again in zig-zags, till he arrives within 150
yards of the crest of the glacis, where his proximity renders
the sorties more serious; then he is obliged to excavate
Demi-Parallels or *Places of Arms,* or portions of parallels
destined to contain a strong guard, to protect the workmen
and quell the musketry of the place, *A, A, A.* (Figs. 162
and 171.) Howitzer batteries, erected at their extremities,
enfilade and ricochet the covered way.

(134) After the second parallel, the flying sap can seldom
be resorted to, because the musketry of the defence begins
to tell, and grapeshot to harass the approaches. It becomes
necessary to advance more carefully, and therefore more
slowly. The zig-zags are no longer made by placing several
gabions at a time, but by disposing them one by one. This
Regular Sap is entrusted to Sappers and Miners, organized
in as many squads as there are lines of approach. A squad
consists of eight men.

The head of the sap is covered by a *Sap Roller,* a large
stuffed gabion, 6 ft. long, 4 ft. wide. The three first sappers
work on their knees; the first sapper excavates a trench 18
in. wide and deep, the second widens it to 20 in., the third
deepens the work of the second 18 in., and the fourth widens
the whole trench 10 in.

The Sap Roller is moved onward by means of a stake or

1

ropes, and fixed whilst the first sapper fills up the gabion he has placed. Sap Fagots (or fascines 3 ft. long, 9 in. in dia-

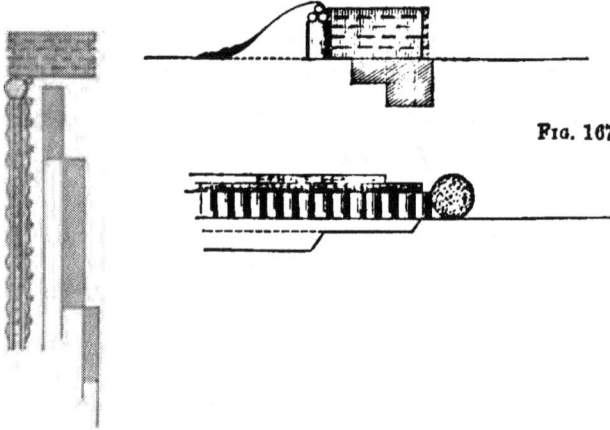

FIG. 167.

meter) are placed between each pair of gabions to stop the shot. Workmen follow behind who give to the trench its proper dimensions. When finished, their profile does not differ from the flying sap. Under favourable circumstances, this sap advances 20 ft. per hour.

(135) In this manner the approaches are carried in zig-zag

FIG. 168.

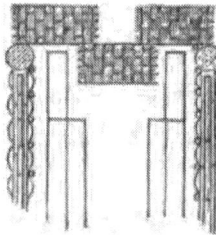

towards the capitals, from the Demi-Parallels; but if their angles become too acute they proceed too slowly, and the besieger must advance in a straight line.* It is done by means of a *Double Sap* (Fig. 168), or two saps advancing close to each other, covered by two sap rollers, united by means of strong poles, to keep them always on the same line. To defilade them they are either made as tambours, or in crochet. (Figs. 169, 170.)

Fɪɢ. 169.　　　　　　　　Fɪɢ. 170.

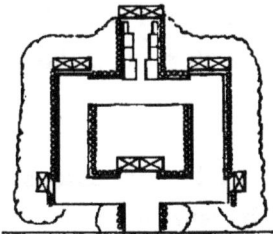 

(136) When the three heads of sap reach the foot of the glacis, they break into single saps on the right and left, to connect their work together, and form the *Third Parallel.*

This is done about the 9th or 10th night. It is not so extensive as the others, it being sufficient to carry it 100 yards on the right and left of the salient attacked. Its extremities are well flanked by the Second Parallel in the rear. It is made wider to receive the guard, whose services may be required constantly. A brisk fire of musketry must be kept up, and for this purpose loopholes formed of sandbags are

---

* When 100 yards of zig-zag do not carry the approaches so much as 32 yards in advance, a double sap is employed.

disposed on the right and left of the sap. Batteries of mortars and howitzers are also constructed, if necessary, to silence the fire of the covered ways. During the execution of these works, the guard of the trenches is placed ⅔rds in the third parallel, and ⅓rd in the second.

(137) From the third parallel the besieger should advance in double sap; but before adopting this measure he avails himself of the slope of the glacis to construct small trenches, called *Circular Portions*, to establish communication between the sap and the third parallel. They are not exposed to enfilade like the saps, and allow a gain of some 20 yards; the double sap thus advances within 30 yards of the crest of the covered way.

(138) The besieger now approaches the momentous period of the siege. To enter the place he must destroy or breach the escarp of the ravelin, and do the same to the body of the place before giving the assault. His batteries must be established in the parapet of the covered way, and to render their construction less dangerous, trenches are excavated to sink the batteries. This sap is called the *Crowning of the Covered Way*. It is made either by regular or by flying sap.

(139) At 30 yards from the crests the double sap falls on the right and left into single saps, describing the head of a T; where they meet the prolongation of the crests of the covered way, redans, called *Cavalier Trenches*, are erected, with three or four tiers of gabions. (Fig. 172.) They are

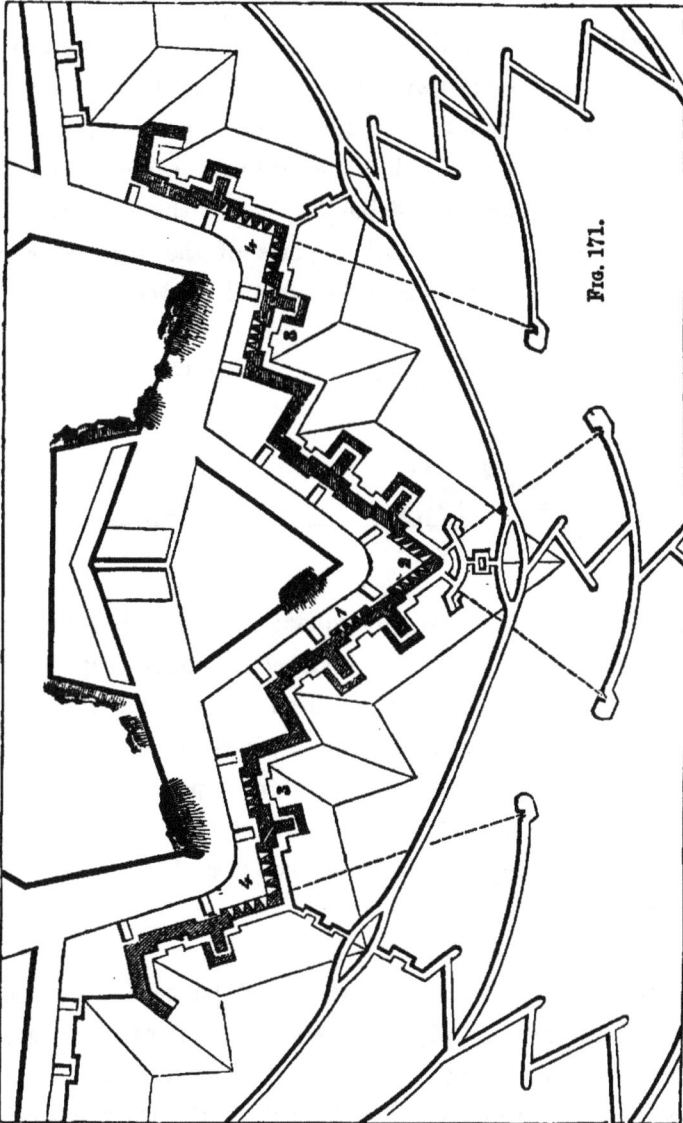

FIG. 171.

formed of two faces at 100°; the first commands the terreplein of the covered way; the second, serving as a mask
against enfilade and reverse fire, to look upon the places of
arms of the bastions.   The relief of these cavaliers must be
such, that the shot may strike the foot of the first traverse
and plunge along the other parts of the covered way.
Marksmen posted on their sides compel the besieged to give

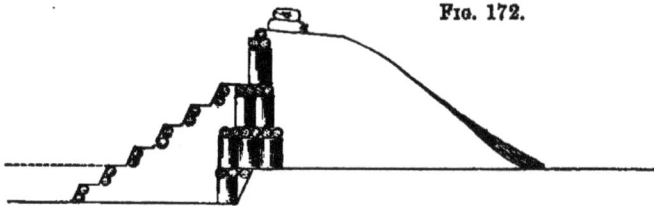

Fig. 172.

up this outwork.   Then two squads of sappers, issuing from
the extremities of the T, advance in double sap to the
salients, and join at six yards from them; there they part
again, to follow the crest on both sides at that same distance of six yards, and the crowning proceeds.   At the
siege of Antwerp (1832), the French did not construct any
cavaliers, but replaced them by batteries of howitzers and
mortars.

(140) When the covered way must be carried by open
force (an operation only to be attempted in cases of great
necessity, on account of its danger), the requisite gabions,
fascines, and sandbags are collected in the third parallel,
besides the usual guard of the trenches, and the workmen,

400 or 500 men per salient, are disposed on their rear. The batteries open a brisk fire, and when they cease, suddenly, at a given signal, the men, clearing the parallels, rush to the covered way, destroy the palisades, and engage the defenders; as, in the meanwhile, the place ceases firing to avoid injuring their own troops, the sappers dispose their gabions according to the direction of the engineer, at six yards from the crest, and begin the crowning. This method is only resorted to when the garrison is not numerous.

This crowning is very dangerous: it must be well preconcerted, to avoid confusion; yet the great accumulation of men on the same point may prove fatal if the enemy can bring a gun to bear upon it. At the siege of Lille (1708), the besiegers lost 6000 men in that operation, and succeeded only in crowning one salient. The Cavalier Trenches, due to Vauban, who employed them for the first time at the siege of Luxemburg, in 1684, are therefore a great improvement.

The crowning is protected against enfilade by traverses and parados; it is successively widened to 24 ft., to place the batteries destined to breach, and also the Counterbatteries destined to silence the flank defence of the ditches.

(141) When the polygon has obtuse angles, the ravelins prevent the besieger from advancing his crowning towards the salient of the bastion; therefore, the ravelin must be taken. To effect this, a *breaching battery* is established on

Fig. 173.

1, and *Counter-Batteries,* 2, silence the guns that flank the ditch of the ravelin.   (Fig. 171.)

(142) On the fifteenth or sixteenth night, whilst the breach is being made, a subterranean gallery, called "*the descent into the ditch,*" is made, to gain access into the ditch opposite the breach.   The slope is regulated according to the height of the counterscarp, so as to arrive 3 ft. below the level of the ditch, in order to be able to enter it.   This descent is a long operation, and delays the besieger.   The breaching batteries were ready on the fifteenth or sixteenth night, and it is not until the twentieth or twenty-first day that the besieger can assault the ravelin.

Fig. 174.

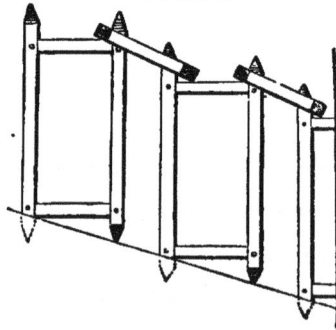

These descents are made in different manners. When the depth is not great, the sapper makes a cutting, which is protected by *Blind Frames* (Fig. 174) covered with earth and fascines; or a few shafts are sunk close to the counterscarp, opposite the breaches; charges are lodged in chambers at their bottom. This explosion will throw in the counter-scarp, and the ruin joins that of the breach.

Sometimes the descent is begun by blind frames, and finished by regular gallery.

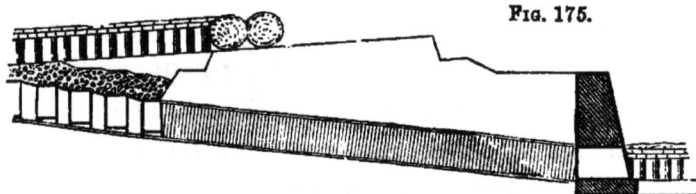

Fig. 175.

(143) When the walls of the scarps have fallen, the breach is made practicable by sending a few shells, until the earth assumes a gentle slope, while some intelligent sapper reconnoitres. Troops accumulated in the crowning are kept ready, and the batteries maintain a vigorous fire against the counterscarp, whilst the sapper makes an approach across the ditch, and at a given signal the column of assault descends the gallery, clears the ditch, ascends the breach, and attacks the garrison of the ravelin; whilst the flying sap, following the slope of the breach, insures the future communication. This operation is much like the crowning of the covered way, and may become as dangerous. It is generally preferred to advance regularly in sap

along the breach to form a *Lodgment* or crowning, and by
a fire of musketry to drive the garrison away. Should the
ditch be wet, the descent must open at a little above the
level of the water, and a passage is made by means of
fascines, pontoons, &c., or other means, according to the
views of the engineer.

(144) The ravelin once taken, the besieger finds no
difficulty in pushing the crowning of the covered way to
the salient of the bastion. There again he must erect his
Counter-Batteries (4) to silence the artillery of the flanks
that defend the breach, and his Breaching-Batteries (3).
(Fig. 171). Then, again, a Descent of the Ditch and the
assault on the bastion. This may carry the duration of the
siege to the twenty-third or twenty-fourth night.

(145) This *assault* on the bastion is the most important
operation of the siege; it is for it that all others have been
made, and so many lives have been sacrificed. When all
is ready for its execution, the general entrusted with its
command ascertains that all the communications of trenches,
descents, galleries, &c., are in good condition. The breaches
are reconnoitred, and dispositions are carefully taken to
avoid confusion; the strength of the column of assault, of
the reserves, and of the working party, is determined. A
little before the appointed time, the enfilade batteries and
those of the covered way, keep up a vigorous cannonade,
and once the signal given, the columns, eight or ten files in

front, issue from the trenches, run across the ditch, and
assault with fixed bayonets the defenders of the breaches.
It is advisable to postpone this decisive movement till day-
break. After a success, great care is still necessary; pursuit
must not be thought of, lest some ambush should have
been prepared, and great circumspection must be shown in
taking possession of the ramparts and of the town. During
the assault, the army is under arms, ready to prevent the
garrison from making its escape, or to repel any attempt to
relieve the place.

(146) After the establishment of the third parallel, the
defence confines itself to keeping a fire on the heads of the
sap, and to constructing traverses to resist the batteries of
enfilade. Blinded frames are also found of great utility.
The garrison makes sorties against the sap, destroying and
burning all it can, but they are not so effective as a good
fire from the ramparts.

When the approaches draw near, and there is no longer a
doubt as to the bastions the besieger intends to attack,
interior intrenchments are organized with the utmost speed,
to command the breaches, which is rather difficult in empty
bastions. During the crowning of the covered way, the
artillery must act with its utmost energy; but as it has
been disorganized, mortars are employed, since they can be
placed anywhere, provided they are not out of range.

During the construction of the Counter-Batteries, the

mines, to which we shall devote a few lines in another chapter, may delay the besieger.

The resistance the garrison can offer to the passage of the ditch depends on the number of guns it has succeeded in keeping safe. When the ditch is wet, combustible matters, shells, &c., are thrown on the dams. If reservoirs and sluices have been constructed, it is the time to use them, in order to delay the passage.

The only resource left to the garrison is now to defend vigorously the breaches; there all its energy is called into play; fires are lighted on their slopes, and kept burning by a continual supply of fascines, &c. At night, quantities of crows' feet and broken glass are spread; chevaux-de-frise, abattis, &c., are placed, and barrels of powder and shells are duly prepared to be lighted and rolled on the columns of assault when they reach the foot of the breach. Mines are also resorted to.

(147) If these means prove insufficient, and if no gun has been saved on the flanks, the last resource consists in selecting the most resolute men to charge the assailants. These troops are, if possible, covered with cuirasses. The first rank, armed with long pikes, kneels, whilst the rear rank pours a volley on the enemy; grenades, &c., being thrown upon both sides of the breach by special detachments. Then they charge with fixed bayonets, and the reserve comes to their support. If driven back and pursued

actively, field artillery, kept in readiness, may still check the advance of the besieger.

The defence of the breaches is one of the most important —not to say the chief resource, of a besieged fortress; and a garrison should never give way to discouragement because the ramparts have been battered down; it will still fight at a very great advantage over the enemy, and there are many instances to be found in military history of a successful resistance.

The defence of Rhodes in 1521, besieged by Solyman, shows what a small but determined garrison can do against a much superior foe.

When the Constable of Bourbon had ruined the ramparts of Marseilles in 1544, the breaches were so skilfully and gallantly defended, that the Imperialists were compelled to raise the siege.

At Maestricht, in 1676, a French garrison of 6000 men fought so vigorously for the defence of the breaches, that the Prince of Orange was obliged to give up any further attempt, and to retire with a loss of 12,000 men.

The breaches of Turin (1706) were defended by large fires—and successfully, too.

St. Jean d'Acre was besieged in 1799 by Napoleon, and although the ramparts had been overthrown, all assaults proved unsuccessful, and the French had to retire, leaving their guns behind them.

In many other instances the Turks have given us a

good example to follow, especially in the Russian campaign of 1828.

At Badajoz, in 1811, the English were repulsed at every assault. In 1812, the same place again resisted, and if General Picton had not surprised the Castle of San Cristoval, the vigorous defence of the breaches would again have saved the place.

Even when the besiegers have gained a footing in a fortress, all hope of further resistance is not lost.

Prince Eugene, at Cremona was obliged to retreat; so were the English at Berg-op-Zoom. At Saragossa, in 1809, the French had to besiege almost every house.

(148) The governor of a place cannot capitulate before having resisted at least one assault on the bastion. His honour is at stake. Want of arms and ammunition, or almost complete destruction of the garrison, are the only reasons that should induce him to surrender. The task and responsibility are immense, and none but men of great skill and energy are fit for that post. To prolong the resistance at all risks must be his motto. When all fails, then he must endeavour to obtain good terms, and if they are refused, his forlorn hope is to attempt an evacuation, and to force his way through the investment.

Chapter VII.

Sec. I. SYSTEMS OF VAUBAN.

Vauban, First System.

(149) The line of front, fixed at 360 yds., is a mean between the extreme limits which can be given to permanent fronts, with the relief adopted by Vauban. The minimum (300) is determined by the condition that the entrance of the postern on the middle of the curtain should be seen and defended by the musketry of the flank. The maximum (400) is obtained by the condition that the lines of defence should not exceed the effective range of musketry. Thus 360 is the length of the ordinary or mean front. The

Fig. 176.

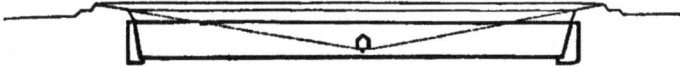

Fig. 177.

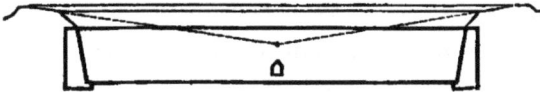

condition of seeing the postern from the flanks is the basis of the alterations made to the relief when the length of the front is imposed upon us. Thus, if the front were only

280 yds., and the relief 44, there would be a dead ditch in front of the curtain; and to remedy this, the relief should be lowered to 22 ft. Thus small fronts give shallow ditches, and long fronts give a bold relief, besides large bastions.

(150) The perpendicular varies from ⅛th to ⅙th.

The flanks are destined to defend the breach, and are counter-battered by the batteries established at the crowning of the covered way of the bastions: the besieger has a space equal to 40 yds.—30, the width of the ditch, added to the 10 of the covered way. To have any chance of resisting these counter-batteries, the flanks should therefore not be less than 40 yds. In the hexagon, the perpendicular ⅙th gives thus 54 yds. If it were made longer, the prepon-

Fig. 178.

derance of the flanks would increase, but the angle of the bastion would become too acute. This latter consideration renders it necessary to shorten it for the square and the pentagon, the angle of these pentagons being smaller. All bastions are thus maintained of a proper size, but the flanks are shortened, and this is a drawback which is obviated by making the ditch somewhat narrower.

(151) The object of tracing the flanks by means of the

circumference is to give a good opening to the angle of
defence; it is equal to 85°. It would have been simpler
and better to draw them perpendicularly to the lines of
defence, as it has been done before and after Vauban (192).

(152) The counterscarp of the main ditch is directed
towards the shoulder-angles of the bastions, to give full

Fig. 179.

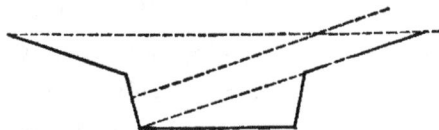

scope to the flanks; if it had been kept parallel, a part
of the defence of the flanks would have been lost.

(153) The purpose of the ravelin is to give a good
flanking fire on the capitals of the bastions, and to command the approach. Its saliency, which is great in polygons of many sides, obliges the enemy to take it before
attempting the assault on the enceinte. The length of its
perpendicular (100 yards) is not however sufficient; and
Vauban, in his later tracing, increased it.

(154) The faces directed to 10 yards from the shoulder-
angles of the bastions, protect the flanks against the
enemy's establishment on the crest of the glacis. Their relief
permits a fire over the glacis without masking the defence
of the place. The ditch opens on the faces of the bastions,

K

to be defended by them, but it is an opening which permits the enemy to breach, and modern engineers have attempted to shut this *trou* of ravelin.

(155) The tenaille is traced on the lines of defence, and has a small relief, not to mask the artillery of the flanks. It can thus give a grazing fire on the terreplein of the ravelin, to prevent the besieger from occupying it, and also an oblique fire on the main ditch.   It covers the revetment of the curtain and of the flanks, and gives in its rear a good space for the defenders to collect in safety. The passage of 8 yards at its extremities, called trou of tenaille, has the defect of enabling the besieger to breach the flank from the crest of the re-entering place of arms.

(156) The Caponier is merely intended to cover the defenders in passing across the ditch from one work to another.

(157) The covered way is made 10 yards broad only, to prevent the besieger from establishing his batteries in its terreplein.   It is, however, sufficient for the occupation of musketry, and for the free circulation of troops.   Its glacis conceals the revetment on the rear, and obliges the enemy to reach its crest before he can make the breaches, and then he has to excavate its crowning to obtain a cover for his batteries, a labour of no small difficulty. This

covered way gives on the approaches a strong grazing fire, without masking that of the works on the rear.

(158) The Re-entering Places of Arms are destined both to permit the garrison to form before making a sortie, and to flank the long branches of the glacis; for this latter reason Vauban made their angles of defence 100°.

In 1697, at the siege of Ath (some authors say in 1688, at the siege of Philipsburg), Vauban used the ricochet fire for the first time; and he afterwards threw up Traverses along the covered way: they are about 30 yards distant, the distance of the flight of a ricocheting ball. Those established at the salient places of arms are placed on the rear of the faces of the ravelin and of the bastions, that they may not afford a shelter to the enemy, and to expose their terreplein to the view of the enceinte.

(159) For ditches destined to contain water, Vauban increased the width from 30 to 36 yards. These wet ditches have the advantage of altogether preventing surprises, and of allowing a reduction in the amount of the garrison. The besieger has no longer an easy access to the breaches; a dam must be constructed, thereby limiting the front of the columns of assault. Two breaches only can at a time be assaulted, and the enemy cannot employ the ditch to place his depôt. On the other side, the communications between the enceinte and outworks are difficult;

they are established at the moment of need by means of bridges, which consume both time and labour, and after all constitute but a precarious communication, since the besieger will not fail to enfilade the ditches. As soon as the crowning of the covered way begins, the garrison can only communicate with the outworks by means of boats concealed in a little harbour reserved at the gorge of the ravelin. The defence is thus rendered less vigorous. In winter the water may freeze, and wide cunettes must constantly be cut through the ice.

Dry ditches possess properties of an opposite character, the communications being safe and almost indestructible; sorties can be made, and the defence assume all its power. Wet ditches will therefore be preferred for small places, dry ones for fortresses well scarped and well garrisoned.

The best plan consists in adopting ditches that can at will become dry or wet; in that case, they are kept wet as long as the besieger cannot attack the outworks; but when sorties become necessary, and when the possession of the outworks is to be disputed inch by inch, water must disappear. The descent into the ditch is then easily submerged; the passage, too, is hindered by chasses (184), &c. If, however, a depth of water of 6 ft. cannot be obtained, it is better to renounce the use of it, inasmuch as it then becomes an impediment for the defenders, without being an obstacle for the besiegers.

Second System.

(160) The rapid progress of the art of attacking fortresses, and especially the discovery of ricochet fire, induced Vauban to modify his tracing. As the loss of the bastion was always followed by that of the town, he transformed the bastion into Counterguards (178), or outworks of the form of a lunette or a redan.

FIG. 180.

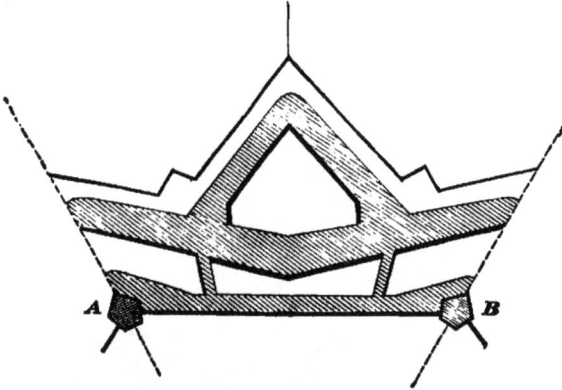

AB being the side of the polygon to be fortified = to 280 yards, he erected at the angles Bastioned Towers, in masonry, to flank the ditch of the enceinte. These towers contained two *Casemates,** or subterranean vaults built

---

* Casemates, from the Spanish, 'casas-matas,' slaughter-houses; thus named because when these subterranean vaults were first employed it was supposed they would occasion great slaughter. The smoke gene-

bomb-proof; the first at 6 ft. above the level of the ditch; each casemate had two guns firing through embrasures on each flank, making altogether eight guns only for the ditch.

Third System.

(161) In his third system, the front AB being, as in the first, 360 yards, he gave an additional defence to the ditch by tracing a bastioned curtain with a perpendicular equal to 10 yards.

In this system the scarps were built of masonry to the level of the ground only, thereby giving a great exterior slope to the parapet. A berm of 10 ft. was reserved at the top of this scarp.

Fig. 181.

This berm has been adopted by some modern engineers,

rally disqualifies them from serving the artillery with any effect, but they constitute good shelter for men and ammunition during a siege.

under the name of *Chemins des rondes,* because it enables the officer on duty to go his rounds, and observe more closely the ditch and covered way. A loopholed wall, 6 or 8 ft. high, is erected on it. This berm renders the breaching

Fig. 182.

of the parapet more difficult, gives a better position to the defenders to repel escalade, and to throw grenades and combustible matter into the ditch; but it affords a good landing-place to a storming-party for turning the work.

In these two systems the expenditure is nearly doubled by the augmentation of the masonry, and this drawback is not compensated by the increase of resistance the tracing gives.

Sec. II. MODERN SYSTEM.

(162) Cormontaingne, a disciple of Vauban, is the author of a system which was first applied in 1728 and 1735 to the forts Moselle and Bellecroix, at Metz. After having received some modifications from modern engineers, it has become known in this country under the name of Modern Front.

Supposing the line of front = 360 yards, the perpendiculars are fixed, as in Vauban, to $\frac{1}{8}$th, $\frac{1}{7}$th, $\frac{1}{6}$th. The faces of the bastion are ⅓rd of the front, 120 yards; the flanks are drawn perpendicularly to the lines of defence.

FIG. 183.

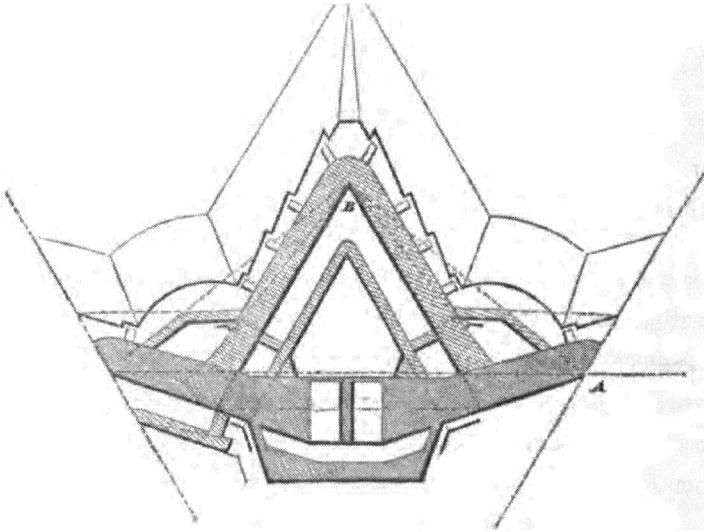

(163) The re-entering angle of the tenaille in Vauban could not be seen from the flanks; to obviate this, a curtain of tenaille is traced parallel to the enceinte at 26 yards; the thickness remains 16 yards, and the extreme profiles are at 5 yards from the flanks; the counterscarp of the main ditch is tangent to circles described from the salients with a radius of 30 yards, and directed on the shoulder-angles of the crests of the bastions.

(164) In order to prevent the besieger from crowning

the covered way of the bastions at the same time as that of the ravelin, Vauban in his last tracings gave a greater saliency to the ravelin. Cormontaingne took its capital, equal to $\frac{4}{15}$ths of the front. Now, 34 yards are taken off from the shoulder-angle of the bastions, along the faces : an equilateral triangle described on this line, gives the ravelin. The ditch is 20 yards wide, the ravelin 20 yards thick. Its great saliency, which increases with the opening of the angles of the polygon, obliges the besieger to take it before crowning the covered way of the bastions, and its reduced thickness prevents him from establishing batteries on the terreplein to breach the redoubt.

(165) Vauban usually placed a redoubt in the ravelin, instead of constructing it with palisades. Cormontaingne gave it a scarp and a ditch. The face of this redoubt is drawn parallel to that of the ravelin from the shoulder-angle of the crest of the bastion. Its ditch is 10 yards wide, its depth is 3 ft. less than that of the main ditch, to prevent the besieger from attacking the ravelin at the gorge. Its gorge is obtained by bisecting the thickness of the ravelin at its extremities, and joining the points of bisection.

The flanks of the redoubt are traced by marking off 20 yards on each face from the point where they meet the gorge, setting 16 yards off on the gorge, and joining. These redoubts must be carried too, before assaulting the bastions, since their flanks (18 yards long, and armed with 4 guns) can give a slanting and reverse fire on the breaches of the enceinte.

The caponier remains as in Vauban.

(166) The covered way is also of the same width, 10 yards. The re-entering places of arms are larger, and contain a redoubt, which renders the attack by vive force impossible.

This redoubt is traced by bisecting the re-entering angle of the counterscarp, and joining the flanked angles of the bastion and ravelin together; the line AB thus obtained gives the counterscarp of one face of the redoubt, the other is drawn from the salient places of arms before the bastion. The scarp is parallel, and at 5 yards distance. The parapet of this face has a flank of 6 yards, to give a fire on the breach of the ravelin; in order to mask the staircase at the gorge, the ditch of the ravelin is enlarged by tracing the counterscarp on the line that joins the extremity of this flank to the salient angle of the ravelin.

The ditch of the face towards the bastion is not flanked— a great disadvantage. In Vauban's system, the besieger could establish batteries in the covered way of the Re-entering Place of Arms, and breach the curtain through the space intervening between the tenaille and the flanks, called *Trous des Tenailles*, thereby obliging the defender to give a great extent to the interior retrenchments (175) constructed to prolong the resistance after the assault on the bastion. With this tracing, the trous des tenailles are masked.

The strength of the redoubts obliges the besieger to advance carefully to the crowning of the covered way of the bastion, and compels him to run a fourth parallel across the slope of the glacis.

(167) The crest of the re-entering place of arms itself is described from the re-entering angle of the counterscarp as a centre, with a radius of 65 yards.

The crest of the salient place of arms is cut off perpendicularly to the capital, to give a banquette of 6 yards, in order to obtain a direct fire on the approach.

The glacis is also 50 yards wide.

(168) The traverses of the places of arms are traced, as in Vauban, 6 yards thick ; along the faces there are two more traverses, 8 yards thick : the crochets are traced in Cremaillère to prevent the besieger from finding shelter in them, as was the case with the crochets of Vauban.

(169) To command the approaches when the ground presents hollows, as well as to form traverses or parados to protect the houses or other buildings in the rear, *Cavaliers*, or works with a great relief, have been employed, in any part of the enceinte. They are generally constructed of earth, and so organized as to form an interior retrenchment.

When such a cavalier is to be constructed in a bastion, its faces are traced parallel to those of the bastion, and 34 yards within them; the ditch is 10 yards wide. The crests of its faces are parallel to, and at 10 yards from the cordon, and on the flanks at 34 from those of the bastion.

The length of these is fixed by tracing the base of the exterior slope at 10 yards from the crest, and making it 28 yards long.

(170) To transform it into an intrenchment, a *Coupure* is made on the face of the bastion at the point where the breaches can be made. Its counterscarp is drawn perpendicularly to the face of the bastion from the point where they are met by the faces of the ravelin produced.

Its scarp is parallel to, and at 10 yards from it; its crest at 7 yards. To flank the ditch of the cavalier, a traverse is erected on the rear of the coupure, perpendicularly to the face of the cavalier, and 8 yards in the rear of the scarp of the coupure. Its crests are 7 yards and 12 yards long. The length of the parapet of the coupure and that of its traverse are limited by a line drawn from the extremity of the crest to the corner of the counterscarp of the coupure— a method which conceals the staircase of the coupure from the terreplein of the bastion, and insures a safe retreat. (Fig. 184.)

Fig. 184.

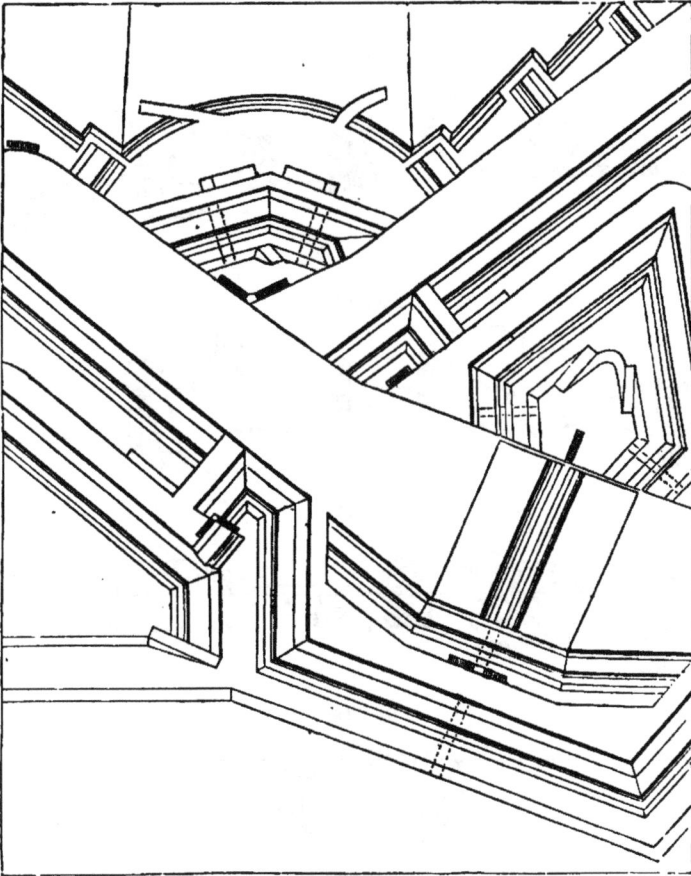

(171) A coupure is also made in the face of the ravelin; its counterscarp is determined by a perpendicular drawn from the extremity of the Re-entering Place of Arms. Its ditch is 5 yards wide.

(172) In the profiles here given (Figs. 185, 186, 187, 188, 189), the line *AB* represents the level of the ground.

FIG. 185.

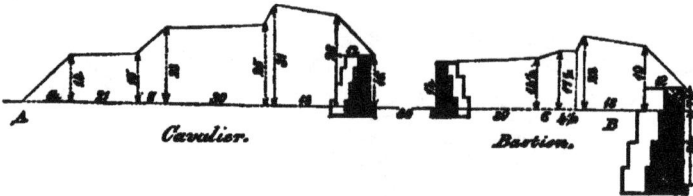

FIG. 186.

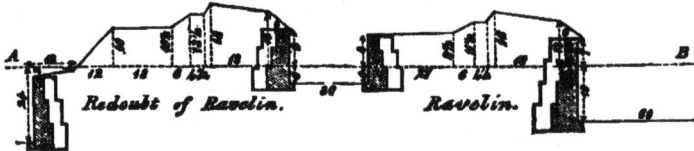

FIG. 187.

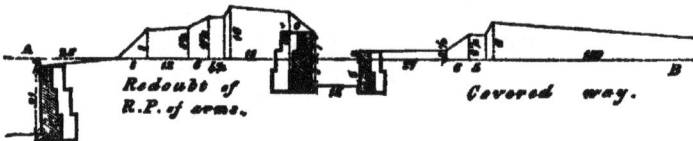

FIG. 188.

FIG. 189.

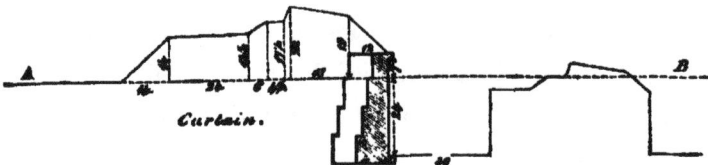

(173) The revetments adopted by modern engineers differ from those of Vauban. A *leaning* revetment

Fig. 190.

(Fig. 190), according to the laws of mechanics, is better than either a sloping or a vertical one, but with the slope in front, this wall is exposed to the action of the weather, and the masonry gets soaked, plants grow in the interstices, &c. To avoid this, the walls are built perpendicular in front and counter-sloping in the rear (Fig. 191), or by steps (Fig. 192), although this requires more masonry.

Fig. 191.   Fig. 192.

Some engineers also advocate the revetment in *Décharge*, where the Counter-forts are connected by arches, which have a greater power of resistance to pressure and to artillery, without much increasing the amount of masonry. The utility of these revetments was made evident at the siege of Dillemburg, where the breaching was almost impracticable.

(174) A Postern forms, as in Vauban, a communication from the interior of the place through the curtain into the Main Ditch. It also passes through the tenaille. Staircases are placed at the gorge of the redoubt of the ravelin, of the tenaille, of the salient and re-entering places of arms.

A Ramp 12 yards long and 3 yards wide leads from the ditch of the Redoubt of the Re-entering Place of Arms to the Covered Way.

The terreplein of the redoubt communicates with its ditch by means of a postern 6 ft. wide.

Ramps 20 yards long and 4 wide lead from the ravelin to the ditch of its redoubt, and a staircase communicates from this ditch with the terreplein of the coupure.

Posterns through the middle of the redoubt of the ravelin lead from its terreplein to its ditch.

The usual ramps are constructed along the rampart, barbettes also are erected at the salients of bastions, ravelins, and redoubts of ravelins.

Two ramps also lead from the rampart of the bastion to the terreplein of the cavalier.

The sally-ports of the Re-entering Places of Arms are of a curved outline, to prevent enfilade.

As in Vauban, and all other systems, a *Cunette*, or diminutive ditch in the middle of the main ditch, serves to drain it.

Sec. III. ADDITIONAL WORKS.

(175) To increase the strength of regular fronts, extra works are usually constructed, according to circumstances and localities.

Interior Retrenchments.—We have already seen in the modern system how a cavalier is transformed into a permanent retrenchment. Its object is to cut off the breach, but as the garrison cannot know previously which front will be attacked, the construction of these works is deferred till the siege operations begin. They are almost impossible in empty bastions, because they are commanded by the parapet of the bastions. Full bastions are thus preferable. The form of these works varies. We give here a couple of outlines.

FIG. 193.

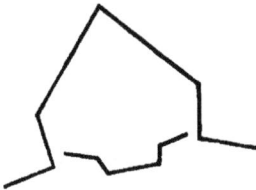

FIG. 194.

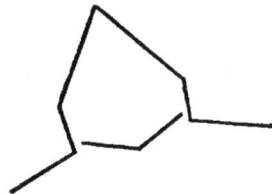

These retrenchments are very important, and modern engineers are almost unanimous in recommending permanent works for their construction. At Berg-op-Zoom, in 1814, the place was saved by the existence of a powder magazine that served as an interior retrenchment, and permitted the surprised garrison to rally.

L

(176) Outworks of different kinds, and of an outline similar to those which we have remarked upon in Field Fortification, are added to prolong the defence, to include an adjoining plateau or bridge, or to command the approaches, or even to give additional space for the garrison.

Hornworks.

Fig. 195.

Fig. 196.

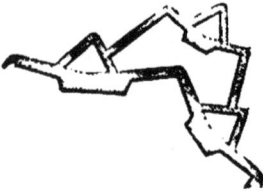

Fig. 197.

Crownworks. (32, Fig. 87.)

(177) *Tenaillons* and Demi-Tenaillons are employed to strengthen the small ravelins of the first tracings.

Fig. 198.

Fig. 199.

Fig. 200.

(178) *Counterguards* or Couvre faces are thrown up before the bastions or ravelins, as we have seen in the second and third systems of Vauban. Sometimes they have a narrow terreplein, and are either scarped with masonry, or entirely of earth.

Fig. 201.

Vauban gave a great thickness to his counterguards, whilst other engineers—Cormontaingne, Bousmard, Carnot, &c.—made them very narrow, to prevent the besiegers from availing themselves of their terreplein to construct the breaching batteries. Experience, however, decidedly pronounces in favour of Vauban's ideas, who recommended not to assault these works, but to destroy their parapets, in order to permit the breaching batteries of the covered way to batter down the enceinte. If the counterguards are employed as a mask to cover the enceinte, a great thickness is certainly desirable, and the besiegers would not save time in assaulting them for the purpose of constructing new batteries in their terreplein.

At the siege of Landau, in 1703, Marshal Tallard lost time in assaulting the counterguards, and was thereby obliged to encounter the Count de Nassau; and had he not succeeded in beating him at Spire, the consequences would have been most disastrous; whilst the breaches to the enceinte could have been made at once, by merely giving an extra relief of 3 ft. to the batteries of the covered way.

At Turin, in 1706, La Feuillade made the same mistake, and not only lost the place, but was beaten by Prince Eugene.

A similar mistake of carrying successively every enceinte, whilst they could be simultaneously breached, was made by Wellington at Burgos in 1812, and he was compelled to retire after five murderous assaults.

(179) Advanced lunettes are occasionally erected. The first instance of their employment occurred at the siege of

Fig. 202.

Luxemburg in 1684, where a lunette delayed five days the crowning of the covered way.

(180) An Advanced Ditch is sometimes placed before the glacis, especially when there is a want of earth for the construction of the ramparts and parapet; and in marshy

Fig. 203.

countries, where the ditches cannot be excavated to a great depth.

(181) *Citadels* are small forts erected in the most inaccessible part of a place, to serve as a refuge for the garrison, in order to prolong the defence after the place has fallen. Should the citadel be constructed on a side of the fortress, its exterior fronts must be very strong, to prevent the enemy from attacking it at first.

(182) Detached Works, either forts or redoubts, are very useful to protect a fortress against bombardment; they may prolong the defence of a place, by obliging the enemy to carry them regularly, or even by inducing him to abandon an attempt to attack in their vicinity.

(183) *Retrenched Camps* before fortresses were proposed by Vauban in 1696. He had found that towns were too confined in space to receive garrisons of any importance,

and as it often happened that armies were compelled to seek a momentary refuge against a superior foe without intending to abandon the country entrusted to their defence, he provided for it by constructing retrenched camps around the places.   It was thus that he erected those of Dunkirk, Ath, Namur, and Lauterburg.   This camp serves as a barrier against invasion, extends the defences of the fortress, allows the besieged to refuse battle without losing ground, offers safe magazines, affords shelter to a defeated army, serves as a place of security for materials, cattle, and forage, and by its great development and resources compels the enemy to attack it regularly.   The Marquis de Feuquières, in his Memoirs, gives long rules for the selection, establishment, &c., of retrenched camps, and mentions those of Utrecht, Brissach, Liège, &c.

The intrenchments which surrounded them were at first continued lines, and it is only at a later period that a positive advantage was derived from these camps, by defending them with detached works which allow the troops to assume, at a moment's notice, the offensive or defensive.   In fact, this improvement was most necessary : in his Memoirs, Frederick the Great, when speaking of the camp of Pirna, said that if it were difficult to carry it, it was not less difficult for the defenders to leave it, and he preferred making use of lines of redoubts disposed on salient and re-entering angles, a method that had already been adopted by Marshal de Saxe, at Maestricht, in 1748.   At the present day, engineers do not entirely agree as to the precise form and nature of these camps; their necessity has been admitted, but their modes of construction differ, and every country adopts a particular system. In France, they have around Paris and Lyons a retrenched camp, the works of which are detached forts. In Austria, at Lintz they consist of towers disposed circularly. The protection and support they ought to give to active forces is greatly relied upon, but before deciding on this question we must wait for experimental proof.

(184) Water can likewise be employed as a powerful auxiliary for the defence, either to form inundations, as we have already seen in field fortification, or to fill the ditches of the place, where water can be had plentifully.

The dry ditches are separated from the wet ones by means of a batardeau; in this, sluices are placed to permit the sudden inundation of the dry ditches, and to form a strong current or *chasse*, which greatly impedes the passage of the besieger. If all the ditches are wet, water can be maintained at different levels, by means of these batardeaux, and sluices will also regulate the chasses. Water may also be employed by the attack; instances are to be found at the sieges of La Fere (1595), of Ceverden (1593), of Brunswick (1606), &c. At Landau (1793), the allies had also intended to turn the river Queich to advantage.

(185) *Mines and Counter-mines.*—Before the invention of gunpowder, *Mines* were excavations or galleries under the walls of a fortress; the foundations were supported by props,

and when completed, the excavation was filled with dry wood, and the timber set fire to. The props being burnt, the walls gave way and opened a breach. The defenders also excavated *counter-mines* to overthrow the machines of the besieger, and to prevent him from executing his mines.

It was in 1503, that powder was first employed for this purpose, by Peter Navarro, at the siege of the Castel del Uovo, at Naples. Many systems of counter-mines have been proposed; we shall confine ourselves to giving a general idea of their construction. Coulon, de Vallière, Belidor, Cormontaingne, Delorme, De Rugy, Mouzé, Marescot, and several engineers, have proposed different systems, which the limits of this work prevent us from passing in review.

They are usually placed at a moderate depth below the surface, and consist of Magistral or *Counterscarp Galleries;* of a gallery parallel to it, called *Envelope Gallery*, connected with the former by galleries of communication; and of *Listening Galleries*, pushed from the envelope gallery towards the country. (Fig. 204.)

They are constructed in masonry, and dispositions are made to prevent the besieger from passing freely among them if he once succeed in entering; they should not extend further than the foot of the glacis, because it is difficult to breathe at 50 yards from the entrance.

From the listening galleries the miner issues by small branches to go and place "chambers" under the batteries, parallels, and saps, as well as to attack the mines of the besieger. The latter are obliged to sink shafts, and to excavate galleries and branches in search of the counter-mines. A subterranean war then takes place, which the limits of this work do not permit us to treat of.

FIG. 204.

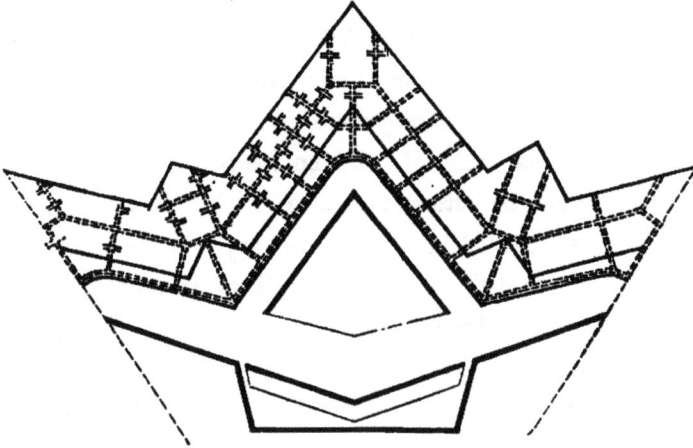

Mines are also employed for the attack and defence of the breaches.

In the explosion of a mine, the radius of the funnel or crater it forms depends on the charge of powder. The distance from the charge to the nearest surface where the crater is to be formed, is called the *Line of least resistance*. An ordinary charge produces a crater of a radius equal to the line of least resistance, or one and a-half. A *two* or *three-lined* charge gives a two or three-lined crater, or a crater of a radius equal to twice or thrice the line of least resistance.

A *Globe of Compression* is a mine loaded with a very great charge of powder. They were employed for the first time at the siege of Schweidnitz, in 1762; the Russians employed them advantageously at Brailou and Varna (1828). They are most destructive to the galleries of the defence, when the latter present their flanks to the besieger.

To find the charge of powder for a common mine, an approximate method consists in expressing in feet the line of least resistance, and in taking one-ninth of its cube for the charge in pounds; according to the nature of the soil this quantity must be altered; thus in rock it must be doubled, and even trebled in strong masonry. An undercharged mine, intended to break a gallery or stop the counter-miner, without breaking the surface of the ground, is called a *Camouflet*.

The construction of these galleries, shafts, &c., the charging, tamping, and firing the mines, constitute the art of the miner, and cannot find place here.

CHAPTER VIII.

OF DIFFERENT SYSTEMS.

(186) The system of Vauban, and the Modern System, are, as we have said, types destined to guide the Engineer, for it seldom happens that a fortress can be regularly fortified according to these rules. The accidents of the ground would render it impossible. The difficulty consists in applying judiciously the principles above mentioned, according to circumstances.

Modern engineers have improved the old tracing, as far as localities would permit, by the construction of new works; and to understand these, we must glance at the chief systems anterior to Vauban.

(187) The *Italian System,* due to San Micheli de Verona (1528), is the most ancient. The front is divided into six equal parts; the flanks are perpendicular to the

Fig. 205.

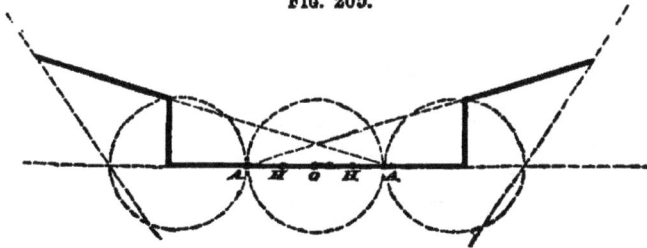

curtain, and equal to one of these parts. (Fig. 205.)   The faces are obtained by joining the extremities of the flanks to *A* for the hexagon, to *O* for the heptagon, and to *H* for the octagon.   Castrioto, in 1584, adopted a tracing very similar to the 2nd or 3rd of Vauban.

(188) In the *Spanish System* the construction is the

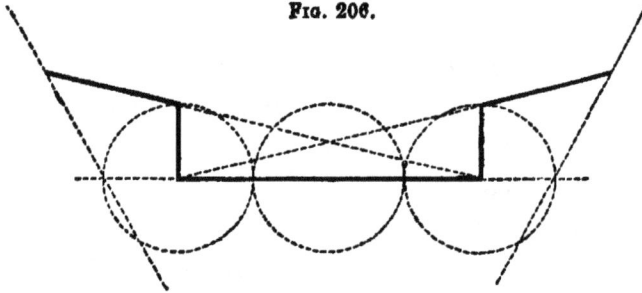

FIG. 206.

same, except that the lines of defence are directed on the extremities of the curtain.

(189) In the *Dutch System*, due to Samuel Marolais, the

FIG. 207.

angle of the bastion varies with that of the polygon. He made it $\frac{1}{4}$ that of the polygon $+15°$ for the octagon,

$\frac{1}{3}$,, $+18°$,, hexagon,

$\frac{1}{4}$,, $+20°$,, heptagon.

At 6 yards in front of the enceinte, he placed a fausse-braie, or second enceinte, as seen in the profile. Its small relief

FIG. 208.

renders the escalade easy; its defenders are injured by the enemy's shot striking the upper revetment and detaching splinters. The besieger having once cleared the fausse-braie, can circulate easily round the whole of the enceinte, and give the assault on several points at the same time.

(190) In France three Systems were employed before Vauban:

1. *Errard de Bar-le-Duc*, in 1594, gave 90° to the salient angles of the bastions, made the flanks perpendicular to their faces, and transformed $\frac{2}{3}$rds of their length into Orillons. The ditch was 26 yards wide at the shoulder, and 30 at the salient. (Fig. 209.)

This system, which it is impossible to apply to high polygons, is very defective.

The orillons mask the curtain, the defence of the ditch is oblique, and the ditch itself is traced on wrong principles.

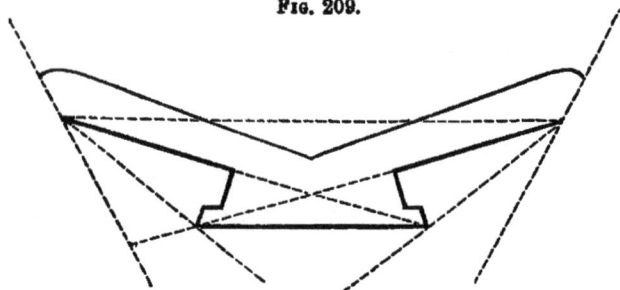

(191) 2. The *Chevalier de Ville*, in 1629, modified the Italian system; he added orillons to the flanks, and constructed a second flank at 14 yards in the rear of the former one.

Fig. 210.

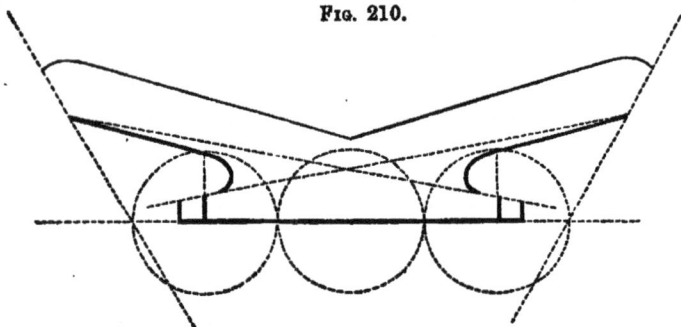

(192) 8. *Count Pagan*, in 1646, greatly improved the science of fortification, and prepared the way for Vauban. For a front of 312 to 390 yards the perpendicular= 58 yards,
　　　　,,　　　295 to 312　　　　　　,,　　　　40 yards.
The faces equal $\frac{3}{10}$ths of the front. The flanks are perpendicular to the lines of defence.

Fig. 211.

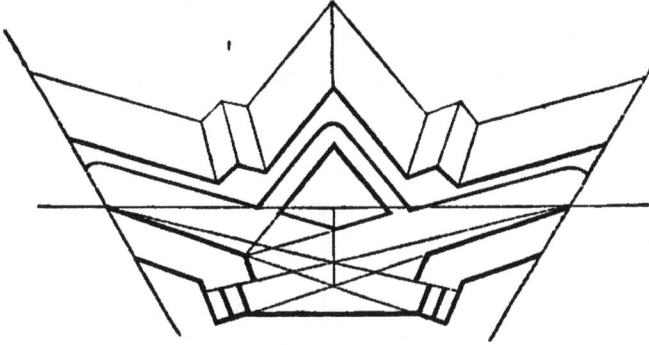

The ditch, 30 yards wide at the salient, is directed on the shoulder-angle of the bastions.

He traced an interior retrenchment in the bastion at 32 yards' distance; he also established three flanks—one at the level of the ground, the 3rd on the level of the interior bastion, and the 2nd of an intermediate relief; but the splinters of the upper scarps so much disturb the defenders of the lower flanks that they do not constitute an improvement. His example has been followed by modern engineers, who have adopted a double flank to pour a greater fire on the counter-batteries.

(193) We might here mention the method which Vauban first adopted before arriving at the First System we have described.

The importance of keeping a few guns in hand for the defence of the breach had induced him to spare the orillons of De Ville, which, however, he soon after modified, as seen in the annexed diagram, so as not to mask the curtains; and to give to the flanks, the importance of which he appreciated, their original length, he traced them on a curved line.

FIG. 212.

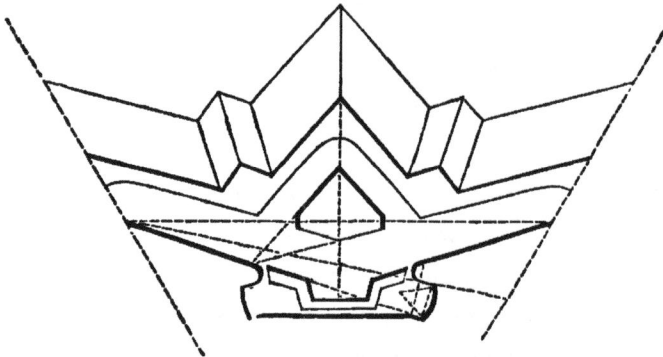

The first ravelin he constructed had flanks, but since they could not defend the breach of the bastion, as the besieger must carry the ravelin before he establishes his batteries, he suppressed them

(194) *Coëhorn*, a Dutch engineer, a contemporary of Vauban, is the author of three systems, the first of which only we shall allude to.

It was intended for marshy countries where water is to be found at 4 ft. below the surface. His chief principle was to cover and flank. The line of front AB for a hexagon is 300 yards, the curtain is 150, and the capital BC is equal to 150 yards. The shoulder-angle is obtained by an arc described from the angle C as centre, and the distance CF as radius. These faces have no escarp, the foot of their exterior slope is at the level of the water.

Fig. 213.

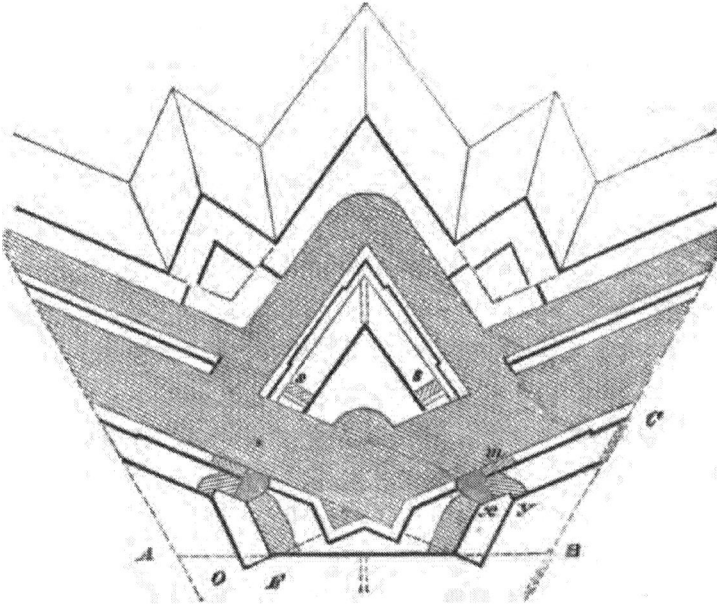

At 32 yards in the rear is an interior bastion with an escarp of masonry, and a belt of palisading at its foot. The flanks of both bastions have a stone revetment, and are connected with the curtain, which has also an escarp.

A tower of masonry is placed on the shoulder-angle of the bastion to flank the dry ditch of the interior bastion.

A wet ditch, 12 yards wide, surrounding the tower, is flanked by a casemate, *m*, and isolates the face of the exterior bastions.

In xy are two bridges giving access to the dry ditch and to the palisaded way.

The curtain FO is casemated for the defence of the terreplein of the flanks. The tenaille with flanks is of earth. The main ditch, 48 yards wide, is parallel to the faces of the bastion, and its counterscarp has no revetment. The capital of the ravelin is equal to 110 yards, and the opening of its angle is 70°. The exterior slope, as in the enceinte, reaches the water; a redoubt with escarp is placed 32 yards in the rear; its ditch is defended by coffers, or casemates, *s s*. Counterguards of earth, 18 yards wide, cover the bastions.

The covered way is 24 ft. wide, and its re-entering place of arms has a redoubt with traverses.

The faces of the bastions and the salient of the ravelin contain casemates for musketry.

A system of posterns and caponiers establishes the communication between these different works, whose strength is increased by a complicated palisading.

This system is capable of a much more vigorous resistance than Vauban's, and requires a powerful artillery; for many soils it is much superior to other systems of the last century.

(195) *Bousmard*, a French officer (1808), attempted

to neutralize enfilade fire by describing curved bastions and curved flanks—a defective plan, since it gives unflanked ditches. He narrowed the main ditch to 10 yards, in order to bring the covered way within reach of hand-grenades,

Fig. 214.

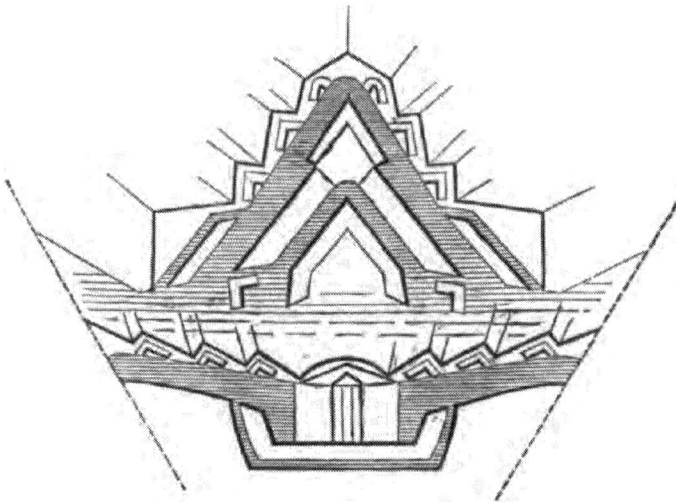

and his traverses were like so many separate intrench-ments, having each a separate staircase leading to the ditch. The tenaille had a relief nearly equal to that of the flanks, in order to cover the latter, and had casemated flanks to contain four guns for the defence of the ditch. The ravelin, containing a redoubt, was advanced beyond the glacis, and had its own covered way and glacis, thus leaving to the besieger no opening upon the main work,

M 2

and compelling him to attack two ravelins before attempting anything on the enceinte,—the leading and the best feature in this system.

(196) General *Chasseloup Laubat,* entrusted by Napoleon with the task of fortifying Alexandria, followed these ideas

Fig. 215.

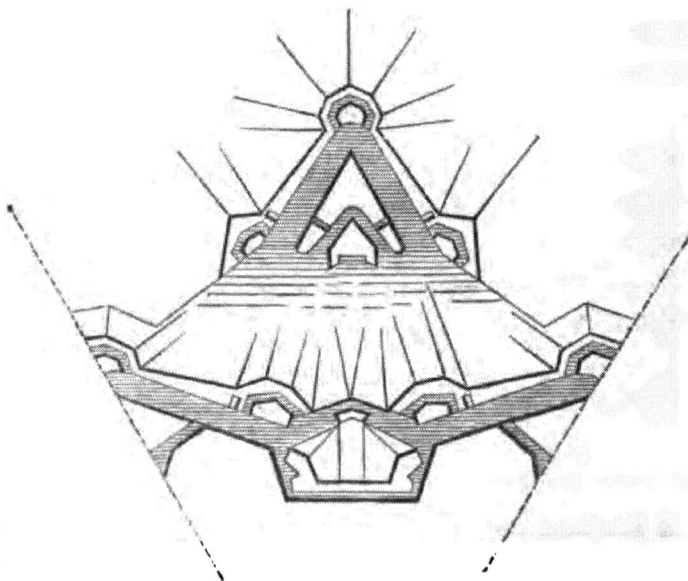

of Bousmard, but did not adopt the curved outline for the enceinte, nor the system of traverses alluded to.

(197) Among the most recent methods we may here

mention that of *Dufour*, a Swiss General, who adopts the tracing of the modern system for the enceinte and the covered way; at the salient of the ravelin he constructs a cavalier with a command of 28 ft. over its terreplein, and shuts the opening of the ditch by producing the inner faces of the redoubt of the re-entering place of arms to the rear of the ravelin. The flanks of the redoubt of the ravelin are suppressed, and replaced by a loopholed wall. The breach in the enceinte can no longer be made from the crowning of the covered way.

(198) *Montalembert*, in 1776, proposed to abandon the bastioned outline, and adopt the tenaille tracing, and to convert the place into an immense battery. The enceinte is formed of a series of re-entering angles en tenaille, flanked by casemated caponiers, CC (Fig. 216), three stories high. A cavalier, H, occupies the curtain, and a counter-guard, L, the salient angle of the polygon; and between these a casemated battery of three stories, KK, flanks the caponier.

These caponiers and the salients are covered by counter-guards with casemated flanks, OO. In front of these casemates are ravelins, also with casemated flanks, VV, and a glacis with covered way.

In the rear of the inner counter-guard is a tower, T, of masonry, forty feet in diameter and four stories high, intended to serve as an interior retrenchment.

All these works are armed with 480 guns, and can cover

Fig. 216.

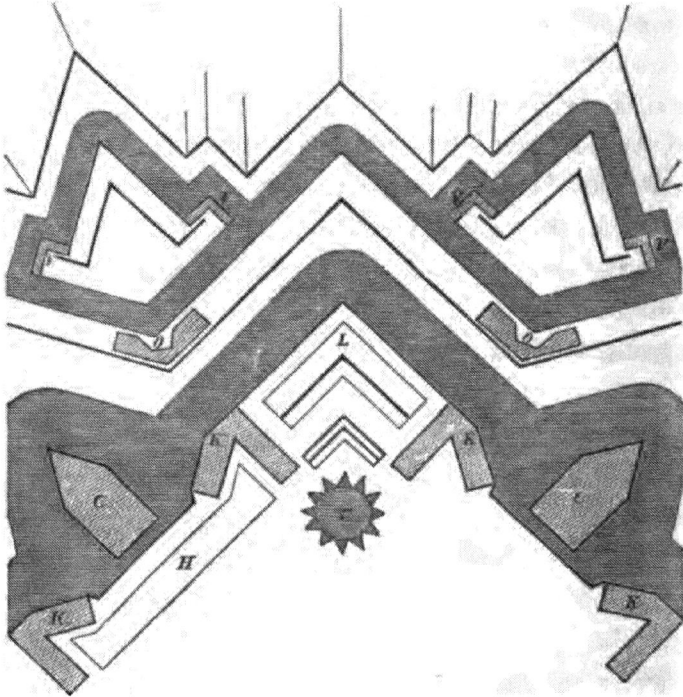

the approaches with a shower of projectiles; but the expenditure of masonry is enormous, and these casemates can be destroyed from a distance by the enemy.

(199) *Carnot*, leaving the defence to vertical fire and powerful sorties, follows the tenaille trace.

The enceinte is formed of a loopholed wall, flanked by casemated batteries, *C*, and is covered by another enceinte,

Fig. 217.

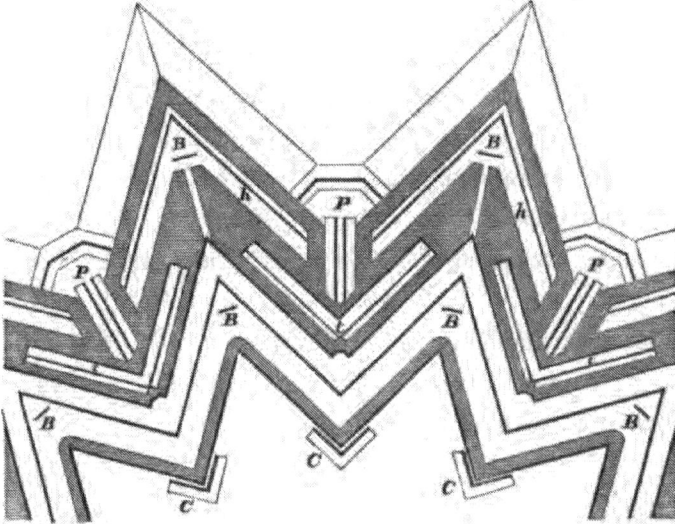

furnished with a parapet, a wall, and a chemin des rondes Tenailles, *t t*, 24 yards wide, are placed in the re-entering angles, and counterguards, *h h*, in earth, of the same thickness, occupy the salients.

The glacis, C, is countersloping, and its places of arms, *P*, are connected with opened caponiers.

Fig. 218.

The salients are occupied by bomb-proof chambers for

mortars, *BB*, firing at each round 150 shells of one pound, and intended, according to the views of Carnot, to render the approach of the enemy next to impossible.

But experience has since shown that this fire of light projectiles is not dangerous. The countersloping glacis is only useful for powerful garrisons, and even then may become dangerous with an enterprising enemy; and the enceinte being continued, a breach at a single point will be sufficient.

The ideas of Montalembert and Carnot have not been adopted by their countrymen, but in Germany they have given rise to a new system.

(200) *German System.*—The line of front is 500 yards

Fig. 219.

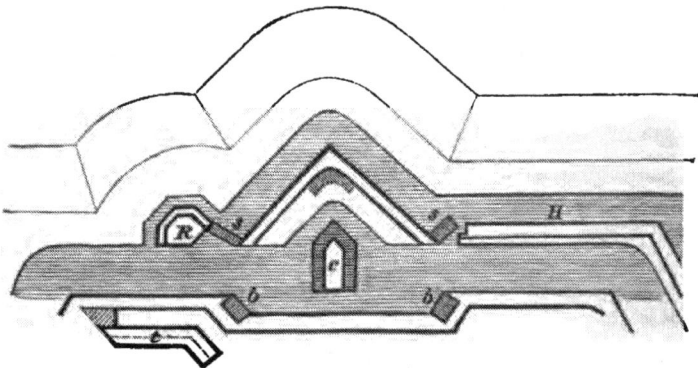

long, and is defended by a casemated caponier, *C*, the salient of which is somewhat less than 90°, and its flanks are 30 yards long. Its faces are flanked at right angles by case-mated batteries, *b b*, 30 yards long, which give to the curtain the bastioned form. This work is sometimes con-nected with the curtain, but when it is an outwork, its gorge is closed by a wall. It is always covered by a ravelin or counterguard 20 yards thick. The main ditch is directed on the shoulder angle of the caponier. The ditch in the front and the rear of the ravelin is 20 yards wide, and opens into the main ditch.

The enceinte is sometimes covered by counter-guards *H*, or by little casemated redoubts, *R*, with a ditch.

The glacis is counter-sloping. The opening of the ditches of the outwork is shut by casemated traverses, *s s*.

The profile of the enceinte (Fig. 218) is nearly the same as that of Carnot. Casemated batteries are established at the salients of the enceinte and of the ravelin, and numerous casemates, *t*, are erected for the lodgment of the troops.

This system varies in Prussia, Austria, &c., but the principle is the same. The flanking defences are entrusted to casemated caponiers, which can be destroyed from a distance from the very beginning of the siege, the glacis, as seen by the diagram, presenting no serious obstacle. The same could be said of the walls of the enceinte, which can-not be protected by the counter-guards against a pitching fire.

(201) It is now time to forewarn military students of a

mistake into which they may easily be led. It is not in learning how to draw a great number of systems that they will acquire useful information. Let them peruse the details of several sieges, for this, above all, will benefit them. It would indeed be a difficult task to stuff one's memory with the never-ending systems daily proposed. If they are not contented with those we have passed in review, let them examine those of Blondel (1683), Landsberg (1712—1758), Sturm (1720), Glasser (1728), Rosard (1731), King Augustus II. (1737), Belidor (1740), Filey (1746—1762), Chiche (1767), Virgin (1781—1788), Roveroni (1794), Noizet Saint Paul (1810), Haxo (1825), &c., &c.; but they will soon be tired, for they will perceive that they are not so much distinguished from each other by any essential difference as by the authors' names. Every one who has written on Fortification has given at least one system of his own; three, however, is the favourite number. Marchi, an Italian engineer, in 1599, has indeed, in a folio book, offered 161 different constructions, which he declares to be his own, and laments the loss of others that were stolen from him!

Engineers, officers, architects, professors of mathematics, students, and even pupils, all have claimed to be masters of an art, the elements of which they did not possess. The claim was easily set up, since by taking the straight line and the curve, an infinity of combinations are to be made. Some fancied that by multiplying the flanks they would attain their object; the most moderate proposed three

flanks, Blondel four, Rusenstein six, &c. Some will have
two enceintes, others cut their works into a quantity of
small parts, hoping to strengthen the system by increasing
its complexity. They all forget the cost, the force of the
garrison, and the provisioning, and each will assert that
a fortress constructed according to his system is im-
pregnable.

The outline of a system is undoubtedly an essential
point, but it is not all. A determined garrison, ably
commanded, will perform wonders even behind a wretched
outline. Metz, in 1558, had but a single wall and rampart, and a dry ditch without bastions, yet Charles the
Fifth, with 100,000 men, could not take it. The Castle of
Mouzun, in Arragon, a mere barrack, garrisoned by only
100 French, resisted (1814) 3000 Spaniards for four
months and a half! Vienna, in 1683, resisted three months
the efforts of the Turks; Candia stood out against them
ten years; Silistria with a Mussa Pacha, and Kars with
a Williams, are still in every one's mind. Let us therefore
beware of placing implicit confidence in any of the systems
alluded to, and instead of attempting to build new fortresses, let us begin by improving the old ones, whenever
necessary.

(202) In Fortification, what we require is not a mere
figure or a combination of lines—the attack, as we have
said, has had an advantage over the defence ever since the
discovery of the ricochet fire; but in the most recent sieges

we have seen the defence assume a greater power than has hitherto been witnessed—not because the outline was new, but because new *ideas* were adopted.

As we observed in 1855,* and as it has been pointed out elsewhere,† a French engineer—Colonel Choumara, in a work entitled *Mémoires sur la Fortification*—has opened a new era in the defence of fortresses; and it is because the Russians have, knowingly or not, adopted his views, that Sebastopol stood so long the efforts of the most powerful battering-train ever brought into the field.

This work has not been translated, and should it be, but few officers of the line could thoroughly understand its contents, and appreciate its great value, through want of knowledge of that branch of mathematics on which the drawing of plans is based. To those of my readers who are already conversant with military drawing, and who are acquainted with the elementary principles of Fortification, we cannot too strongly recommend a serious perusal of these *Mémoires*, for the science at the present time does not extend any further.

(203) Instead of offering a new system, as his predecessors too often did, Choumara proposes new and general principles, applicable to all the systems either past, present, or to come.

The two chief principles are:

---

* *Morning Post*, Dec. 8th, 1855.
† Major Straith's *Fortification*, Appendix H.

1st. The reciprocal independence of the parapets and the scarps.

2nd. The construction of an interior glacis in the ditches.

The first is most prolific of consequences. The walls become a mere safeguard against escalade; they constitute the invariable part of the tracing, the rest of which varies according to the circumstances. When the besieger advances and attacks, the defence counter-attacks him and checks his progress by the erection of new earthworks. In fact, the walls are the mere enclosure of a field of battle, where all the advantage is on the side of the garrison.

The limits of this elementary treatise do not permit us to show the development of this idea. We shall content ourselves with a view of its consequences.

The parapet being removed to the rear, a chemin des rondes, R (Fig. 218), is obtained, and the breach of the escarp is not followed by that of the parapet.

The flanks can be lengthened and nearly doubled, so as to overpower the counter-batteries.

Fig. 220.

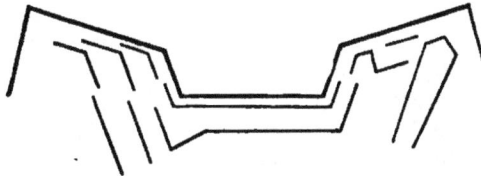

In the bastions and ravelins the effects of the ricochet are almost reduced to nought.

Fig. 221.

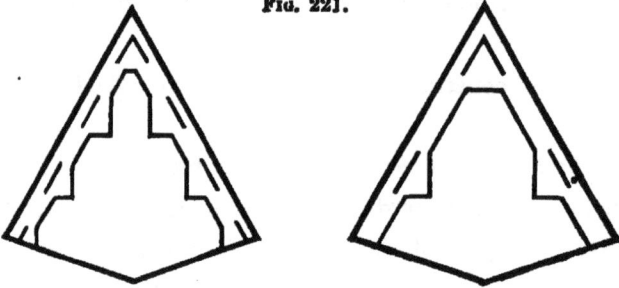

Fig. 222.

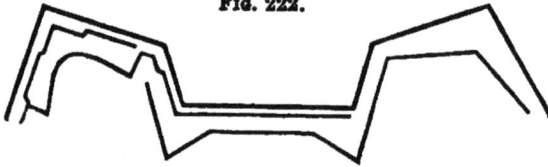

Additional flanks, if needed, can be added.

Fig. 223.

Fig. 224.

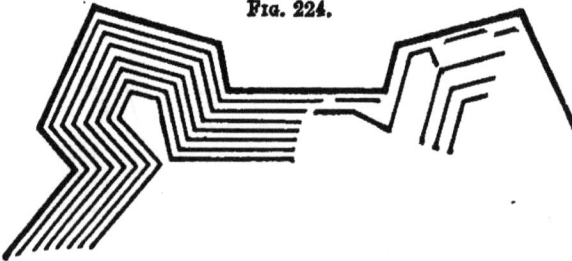

Double enceintes can also be formed.

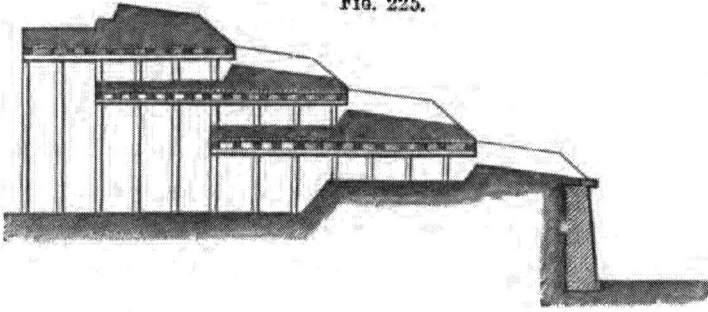

Fig. 225.

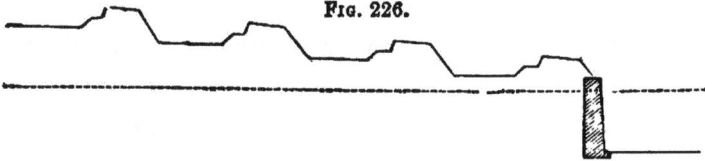

Fig. 226.

Guns can be established on several tiers.

The bastions adjoining the front of attack can join in the defence, &c. &c.

The construction of an interior glacis in the ditch is also a most important discovery. The openings of the ravelin

Fig. 227.

Fig. 228.

and tenaille no longer exist; the breaching of the escarps becomes a most difficult operation; the water-manœuvres rendered most easy assume a great vigour; &c. &c.

(204) That which distinguishes Choumara from other writers on the science, is the objection he has to supersede everything by the introduction of a new system; his constant endeavour is to modify the fortresses already extant, in order to increase their power of resistance. He always affirms that he has no system. In fact he has given principles, deduced consequences therefrom, generalized them; and, although he has grouped together a few combinations susceptible of presenting a formidable *ensemble*, yet he by no means considers them as an indivisible whole; these combinations, he says, can be adopted either partially or wholly, according to circumstances, and the engineer may select the especial improvement required for the particular fortress entrusted to his charge.

(205) Starting from the two principles above mentioned, he leads us to the discovery of various combinations arising therefrom, for the organization of a place from the most simple case, that of an enceinte without either outwork or interior intrenchment, to the most complicated one, that in which, having at disposal both space and money, a complete fortress can be erected, having—

1st. An enceinte, with an interior glacis in its ditch.

2nd. A general intrenchment against an exterior attack,

composed of the combination of the military buildings with bastioned towers, forming themselves good bomb-proof barracks, and so disposed as to favour the interior defence, should the enemy enter the place.

3rd. A ravelin, with a ditch and its interior glacis.

4th. Some redoubts in the salient places of arms of the bastions and ravelins, whose covered way also contains an interior glacis, forming at will a basin of inundation, that is most useful to oppose the construction of the batteries destined to breach the salient redoubts, to submerge the descents into the ditch, the mines, and even the trenches on the exterior glacis, then transformed into a deversoir.

We cannot follow Choumara in all the details he gives. Let it be sufficient to say, that he has rendered to the defence its former superiority over the attack, and that by applying part of these modifications to the old fortresses, the very worst of them evidently become superior to the best tracing hitherto known. To earthworks he chiefly entrusts the active part of the defence; and the recent events in the East speak so loudly in favour of his ideas, that it is needless to dwell longer on their vital and obvious importance.

Although published in 1827, the Memoirs are not yet acclimated in England. As has been the case with every great discovery, some time must elapse before Choumara's ideas become popular. Fortresses are fortunately very seldom erected at present, whilst routine makes us maintain the

N

old ones; when, however, danger shall render some modifications indispensable, or when it may be necessary to construct new places, these masterly principles will undoubtedly be applied, and Choumara will have as great a claim to be called the head of the modern school, as Vauban had during the two last centuries.

CHAPTER IX.

BESIEGING ARMY AND GARRISON.

(206) *The force of a besieging army* depends upon the strength of the garrison, the *morale* of both armies, and the season of the year—elements which cannot form the basis of exact calculations.

In some instances two armies are necessary; one of *observation* to cover the siege, and prevent any attempt on the part of the enemy to relieve; the other to besiege. To this latter army alone we shall direct our attention.

It must provide men for the excavation and guard of the trenches, the construction of batteries, and the investment of the whole circumference of the place; for the police of the camp, the outposts, patrols, extra duties, &c.; also a proper number of sappers and miners, gunners, &c. Supposing the attack to be directed against a front of a hexagon, the First Parallel and its communications on the rear, occupying a development of nearly 8000 yards, would require about 5000 men. But, during the first night, 4800 yards of the parallel only are excavated, and 3000 men are sufficient; and this number will remain the same till the opening of the Second Parallel. This is made by a Flying Sap; and as a man occupies here only 2 ft.,

3000 men will still be required, though the development of the parallel is less. If the batteries for ricochet fire are armed with 50 pieces, at 12 men per gun, that makes 600 men; to guard the trenches, the force must at least be equal to that which the besieged can bring in a sortie, only half the number of the garrison, since the workmen can eventually fight, therefore 2000 men. This gives 5600 men, but as they cannot be constantly at work, they must be relieved, and with one day of rest, the force becomes 11,200 men.

For the investment, the posts must be placed out of range at 3000 yards; and as the salients are at about 500 yards from the centre of the place, the posts will be at 3500 yards, giving a development of 21,000 yards. Subtracting the 6000 for the first parallel, already reckoned, there will remain 15,000 yards, which at 200 men per 1000 yards, require 3000 men.

In infantry, the besieging army must thus number 14,200 men. For the artillery, the service of 100 guns implies 1300 gunners, plus $\frac{1}{6}$th for workmen, officers, &c., amounting to 1500. For the engineers, 200 sappers and miners are not too many for the six saps, and 100 for the mines, &c.—total, 300. Cavalry is employed to cover the wings of the attack, and allowing 100 horse for every wing, it implies 600, because they must be relieved.

Thus for the siege of a hexagon garrisoned with 4000 men (207), the besieging army should muster in round numbers 17,000 men, more than four times the garrison.

Although it is a difficult matter to fix any limit for the

force of a besieging army when it has to prepare against the diversions of an enemy, yet it may be said that attempts with a force less than 60,000 men are not likely to prove successful.

In 1793, the King of Prussia required 100,000 to besiege Mayence. The same year, the English and Austrians had 120,000 men before Valenciennes; and the Prince of Coburg besieged Le Quesnoy with 60,000; but the Duke of York could not invest Dunkirk and Bergues with 50,000.

It is true that in 1796 Bonaparte invested Mantua with 20,000 men, half of which were employed in the siege; and that at Saragossa, in 1809, the French had but 35,000 men; but again, at Silistria, in 1854, the Russians had 70,000 men.

(207) A place can always be defended, whatever be its *garrison*, yet it is advisable to find a minimum, in order not to waste troops that could be more usefully employed in the field.

We suppose the troops divided into thirds: one third on the front of attack, one third at bivouac, and one third at rest; although towards the latter period of the siege all the garrison is constantly required on the ramparts. When the enemy arrives before the place, the garrison has no other duty than putting the place in a state of defence, and sending out patrols and reconnoitring parties; nor will its service become heavy till the besieger has begun sapping.

The covered way is occupied by infantry, since it cannot be expected that artillery will maintain day and night an incessant cannonade. Now, if there are 60 shots per minute directed against the attack, the enemy cannot remain uncovered; this gives 180 men for the three salients, but they cannot fire constantly, and three times that amount is requisite—viz., 540.

On the fronts of attack sentries are necessary, and a post of 25 men per front gives altogether 50 men, including the two half fronts next to that of attack. To repair the works and throw up intrenchments, we must add at least 100 men. Three ravelins are armed, and giving to each a post of 15 men, it gives 45 men, plus 150 for the ravelin of the front of attack.

For the fronts not exposed to attack, sentries are also indispensable, and 100 men are not too many.

Allowing, with Vauban, 40 guns constantly served, and 8 men and 1 gunner to each, 120 additional infantry are necessary.

Thus, without providing for the interior guard of the place, the infantry should muster 3 × 1085 or 3255.

For the artillery, 40 gunners are constantly required, making 150 men, or 180 including 30 officers, workmen, &c.

Adding for sappers and miners 75 men; for the commissariat 40 men; and the cavalry 100; the total amount of the garrison will be 3660, or about 600 men per bastion. This force could not continue a long resistance, because of the heavy losses.

Great support from the inhabitants cannot be expected; only one-sixth of them are fit for service, and one-eighteenth only can be employed at a time. The maximum of a garrison is determined by the capacity of the barracks, casemates, &c., and by the amount of provisions. A representing the number of rations, and B the strength of the garrison, $\frac{A}{B}$ must be greater than the usual length of a siege.

(208) Although the *Armament* of fortresses is the province of the artillery, a few words may be added to give an idea of its calculation.

Vauban wanted 10 guns per bastion, and 5 mortars or Pierriers, making 90 pieces for a hexagon.

Cormontaingne fixed a minimum of 86, and a maximum of 46 for the same polygon.

To maintain a vigorous defence, modern engineers require about 146 guns on the front of attack, plus 5 guns for each other front, making 176 guns for a hexagon.

Guns . . 75	146; but a place provided with two-thirds of this artillery could still offer a good resistance.
Howitzers 85	
Mortars . 21	
Pierriers . 15	

(209) *The number of guns* necessary to the besieger depends upon so many considerations, that exact figures cannot be given. However, no serious attempt should be made against a front with less than 60 pieces.

During the reign of Louis XIV., the battering trains were more numerous than in the wars at the beginning of this century. At the siege of Namur (1692) the besiegers had 260 guns; at Charleroy (1693), 210; at Turin (1706), 251; at Menin (1706), 116; at Lille (1708), 200; at Douai (1710), 368.

The following table of some remarkable sieges will give an idea of the amount of artillery employed in modern times.

	Defence.	Attack.
Valenciennes (1793) . .	175 . . .	167
Neuss (1794)	200 . . .	40
Breslau (1807)	300 . . .	38
Schweidnitz (1807) . . .	250 . . .	43
Ciudad Rodrigo (1810) .	86 . . .	50
Almeida (1810)	98 . . .	67
Tortosa (1810)	180 . . .	50
Lerida (1811)	110 . . .	40
Tarragona (1811) . . .	337 . . .	66
Badajoz (1811)	170 . . .	54
Antwerp (1832)	145 . . .	149
Varna (1828)	100 . . .	45
Silistria (1829)	238 . . .	88

The battering train at Mequinenza (1810) was only 18; at Badajoz (1812), it was 78; at Ciudad Rodrigo (1812), 70; at Dantzic (1812), 130; at Magdeburg (1812), 100; at Riga (1812), 130; &c. The figures varying much.

The regular trains are now fixed at 178 pieces of ordnance in Austria; 162 in France; 142 in Prussia. These figures relate to a serious attack on one front only.

Sir John Jones demands 166 guns :

Twenty-four pounders 40
Eighteen ditto, or heavy howitzers . . 80
Mortars 30
Pierriers 16

Total 166

(210) *The amount of ammunition* required for this ordnance varies very much. At the siege of Schweidnitz (1807), the besiegers fired 1800 projectiles of their own only, and collected 3600 fired by the garrison. At Badajoz (1811), the besiegers had brought before the place 2400 projectiles; yet at the end of the siege they had still 2300 left. At Tarragona, one-third of the balls were provided by the place itself. On the other hand, we see at Dantzic 2200 rounds fired in one day; at Antwerp, 3000; and at Bayonne (1814) Wellington had provided 1750 rounds for every pounder, and from 400 to 500 for other ordnance.

It is generally admitted that 1000 rounds per gun, and 500 per howitzer or mortar, constitute a good approvisionment.

Chapter X.

EMPLOYMENT OF FORTIFICATION FOR THE DEFENCE OF A COUNTRY.

(211) Permanent Fortification is employed for positions which nature has left without defence, or to increase the difficulties which are offered by mountains, rivers, &c. In the preceding chapters we have examined the different means proposed to construct a front on a level surface; it is the part of the engineer to make the best of these systems, according to localities, when ordered to do so. But *when he may be ordered to do so* is a question of very high importance, the solution of which is left to statesmen.

No one will ever doubt the necessity of fortifying a dockyard like Portsmouth, or a town like Perpignan, commanding the road from France to Spain across the Pyrenees; but many sound minds will wonder at the immense number of fortresses to be found on the Continent, and erected, to all appearance, *to no purpose*.

(212) Fortifications have been employed to defend frontiers more by *routine* than from imperious necessity. Systems, too, have been proposed for that purpose. The most ancient plan, which bears the name of Vauban,

although this engineer often complained that too many fortresses were built, is designed to cover a frontier with a triple line of fortified places, with the view of detaining the invader as long as possible with small forces whilst an army is being organized.

At present, however, invading armies are numerous enough to pass between these lines without having much to fear from their small garrisons, and the examples of Holland in 1794, and of France in 1814, lead us to inquire whether this enormous outlay on artificial defences is not altogether useless.

"We have seen the Romans at Trasimene and Cannæ, Hannibal at Zama, Scipio at Thapsus, Sextus at Munda, Melas at Marengo, Mack at Ulm, Brunswick at Jena, defeated, and unable to rally their forces even amidst their fortresses, and close to their capitals."*

In this system, routine had the greatest part. After the struggle of the middle ages, Europe was seen dividing itself into a limited number of kingdoms; these swallowed up the states of smaller importance, enlarged themselves by the addition of dukedoms and earldoms, and sought to establish themselves on strong bases. Of all fortifications, those with which nature supplies are still the best; but every state could not succeed in obtaining for itself such boundaries; even to the present day the coincidence of political with natural divisions is regarded as an impossi-

---

* Montholon, *Mémoires de Napoléon*, tome ii. p. 206.

bility. It happened that to restrain a too warlike nation,—
to keep in check a too powerful country,—the European
states imposed on each other frontiers of an irregular
shape. The consequence was, that in order to protect the
defenceless part of these frontiers and to close the openings,
citadels were erected. Political events changed, and with
them the frontiers advanced or retreated like the tide of the
sea. At every change the same phenomenon took place,
and it is in this manner that the surface of European states
offered so great a number of fortified towns, scattered
without any apparent combination.

In France, Vauban and his successors improved all these
fortresses, and as several lines were found to exist, it was
taken for granted that they were built according to the
regular system alluded to.

(213) It has been said in defence of this system, and it
is still now repeated, that an invading army would not
dare to venture into a hostile country leaving several fortresses in its rear, because its communications would be cut
off. But the invading army is exposed in a limited number
of points only to the combined and therefore uncertain
attacks of the garrisons, each about 6000 men strong. What
may be the strength of the invader? Experience shows
that there is no exaggeration in estimating it at 300,000
men. If this army leaves on the frontier a corps of 50,000 men
to observe the fortresses, their garrisons could not go far off
without exposing themselves to be carried off by a much supe-

rior mass, and there will be still left 250,000 men to march into the interior of the country. But they would not dare do so! Why? The defensive army, already inferior, since it is on the defensive, has been diminished, owing to the necessity of placing garrisons in every fortress,—in *every one*, since it is not known which of them the invader intends attacking. For a frontier of 150 miles, requiring about 21 fortresses, the defensive army loses 125,000 men condemned to remain inactive! If in 1814 Napoleon had not scattered garrisons in Dantzic, Homburg, Magdeburg, Wurtzburg, Glogau, &c., and had collected these forces on the Rhine, they would undoubtedly have delayed, if not altogether prevented the invasion. The great accumulation of fortified places on a frontier has, besides, the inconvenience of entailing a very heavy expenditure on the State. Valuing the mean cost of a fortified town at 600,000*l*., how many millions will be swallowed up by a frontier 150 miles in length? Look at France, which numbered 186 fortresses in 1829, and judge of what she pays for their maintenance alone. Bureau de Pusy said that with the amount they cost he could organize an army of one hundred thousand men.

(214) Modern statesmen have laid aside this system, and proposed new ones. Among the most celebrated we find General Rogniat's method of *Retrenched Camps.** He pro-

---

* *Considerations on the Art of War.*

poses to leave the frontier open, and to entrust the defence of the country to a numerous army, that will find support in a series of retrenched camps resting on fortresses, and distributed from the frontier to the central stronghold, in such a manner that the army could always find one within fifty miles. He intends this army to defend the country while other forces are being organized, checking the advance of the enemy by skilful manœuvres, and driving him to attack the defenders on their prepared ground of the retrenched camps. This system, which has been favourably received, has not yet been put into operation; it is therefore difficult to decide upon it. It starts, however, from a *true principle*—that of entrusting the defence of a country to the *army*, and not to *mere* fortresses. But the invader can also have recourse to skilful manœuvring, and march directly upon the capital, which, according to General Rogniat, is not fortified.

(215) General Duvivier* proposed to have only one place in a country—but an immense one, 40 miles in diameter!—where all the resources of the State are to be accumulated, so as to preclude the idea of ever attempting its attack, whilst the defensive army struggles on the frontier. Unfortunately, before arriving at the realization of this *delta*, the manners, government, &c., of our times must greatly alter.

-----

* *Essays on the Defence of States.*

(216) The method which seems to be adopted now is to fortify the capitals, in order to secure them against a coup-de-main, and to have on the frontier fortresses provided with retrenched camps. In this country, the sea forms a natural defence, and with the construction of batteries and forts around the dockyards and arsenals, it is by many considered as sufficient. Dreamers, however, have not failed to prepare plans for constructing a permanent system of defence by means of fortresses both along the coast and in the interior.

(217) Instead of perusing all these plans, let us conclude with a few remarks.

A system ready-made is like a formula of algebra,* applying to all cases, common sense being sufficient to work it correctly; but in the defence of a country, is a system advisable? Will the invader act exactly in the way foreseen? Will every fortress, line, &c., be called into play? The world of impossibilities daily diminishes, and more especially in war, where almost everything is to be considered as a probability, and provided against accordingly. Alexander, Hannibal, Napoleon, have astonished mankind by the boldness and novelty of their operations; and this may still occur. Therefore let us beware of these systems, ready-made and answering every purpose, and let *common sense* be our guide. The lines of Torres Vedras were a

---

* See General Duvivier.

better defence for Lisbon than any bastioned or tenaille enceinte, yet they were mere field-works.

(218) In this country especially, where an invader is obliged to cross the sea, where military ports are fortified and safe against surprise, there is plenty of time left to prepare field defences of the most formidable description. Let us remember that at present armies are more numerous and more rapid in their movements than formerly, and that a fortress has no influence but on the ground seen by its guns, and that it is only when it is a place situated *there,* and *there* only, *where* the enemy *must* pass, that permanent fortifications are advisable. Let us repeat with d'Arçon,* that—

"At the present day, *professional system* has the effect of spoiling all our ideas, and the poison proves the more dangerous, as it exists without the knowledge of those who are attacked by it, who look upon themselves as only zealously attached to their own art, although they wish by such means to exclude at the same time every other.

"Those who have been advocates for the superiority of the troops of the line, have wished for no other troops besides infantry; the seafaring people have maintained that ships only were necessary; the artillery pretended to be able to protect everything by means of batteries on the coast. Who can say but that the cavalry also, mounted on hippopotami, may not be disposed for defensive manœuvres?"

---

* *Military and Political Considerations on Fortifications.*

The engineers are equally absurd in imagining that nothing but fortifications are needed to insure the quiet possession of a country. Amid this variety of opinions respecting the means to be employed, nothing appears to have been forgotten except the indispensable necessity of *their being all united* and made to *concur* jointly towards the same end.

APPENDIX.

Note I.

PENETRATION OF PROJECTILES.

THE thickness fixed for the parapet depends upon the penetration of the projectiles they are exposed to; it is customary to make the thickness such, that only two-thirds of it can be penetrated.

Instead of giving here the penetration of English ordnance, we deem it more useful to give that of Continental artillery, since it is against it that English troops will have, most likely, to protect themselves.

The following table is the result of experiments made by the French at Metz in 1834. At the distance of 300 mètres (325 yards) the guns are supposed to be loaded with an ordinary charge; at 25 mètres (27 yards), and 1000 mètres (1090 yards), with a strong charge. The dimensions are given in English inches.

		PENETRATION IN								
	Masonry.			Oak.			Earth.		
Distances.	25 m.	300	1000	25	300	1000	25	300	1000
	Inches.	Inches.	Inches.	Inches.	Inches.	Inches.	Inches.	Inches.	Inches.
Guns — 36 pounds	26·77	22·24	12·20	66·85	54·33	31·49	109·05	93·30	69·48
24 "	25·59	20·30	10·82	62·99	45·08	27·55	108·26	77·55	60·82
16 "	22·44	15·15	7·67	54·72	37·40	19·68	96·48	66·53	50·39
12 "	20·89	13·58	6·10	46·06	33·27	14·56	64·96	49·01	35·03
8 "	17·74	11·61	4·18	39·37	28·74	10·62	58·29	43·30	28·74
Howitzers* — 22 centim.	...	...	...	28·34	17·74	9·05	48·42	33·85	23·22
16 "	...	...	...	33·27	20·50	9·84	52·95	35·03	22·04
15 "	...	...	...	27·55	20·11	6·29	44·48	32·67	18·14
12 "	...	...	...	14·96	8·26	3·93	27·16	21·29	10·23
Mortars fired at an elevation of 45° — 32 " } at 600 metres	4·33	4·33	...	...	10·62	...	...	21·65	...
27 "	3·93	3·93	...	...	9·84	...	...	19·68	...
22 "	3·14	3·14	...	...	5·90	...	...	11·81	...

* Shells and bombs are named from their diameter, expressed in centimètres.　A centimètre = 0·39371 inch. The French metre = 39·37079 inches.

The above results must be multiplied—

In masonry, by 1·25, when old.

     „   1·75, when of bricks.

In wood, by . 1·   for beech, yoke elm, ash.

     „   1·3   for elm.

     „   1·8   for pine and birch.

     „   2·   for poplar.

In earth, by . ·63 for sand mixed with gravel.

     „   ·87 for ditto, but lighter.

     „   1·09 for mould, or the above rammed in

     „   1·44 for clay.

     „   1·50 for light soils.

     „   1·90 for ditto, recently rammed in.

Although it may seem idle to recommend making the parapets of sufficient thickness to resist the projectiles they are exposed to, yet this important subject is sometimes neglected in the hurry of the moment. Nothing more discourages the men entrusted with the defence of a work than to find that they are not efficiently protected. During the Seven Years' War, at the siege of Colberg, a cannon-ball came right through the parapet of a battery, and took off the head of a gunner. It is far better to bestow a little more labour to make the parapet too thick, than to fall into the other excess, for this extra trouble will in the end save time. At the first bombardment of Sebastopol, the French had not calculated on the powerful artillery of the Russians, and in a few hours their batteries and powder-magazines were destroyed. Warsaw, in

1832, was defended by earthworks; yet General Paskewich (with a train of 300 guns) soon annihilated the whole.

Earthworks resist better the effects of ordnance than masonry, but it does not follow that they should be exclusively employed. The remarks given in the text (203) show the advantage they possess in the hand of a skilful engineer to counteract rapidly the progress of the besieger, and dispute his advance inch by inch; but masonry has been, and will remain, a very important item in permanent works, whatever its adversaries may say when in their easy discussions on paper they make abstract calculations of the ever-changing circumstances of site, garrisoning, &c.

It may here be added that a few years ago iron was proposed as an exterior revetment by General Paixhans, but several experiments have clearly proved it to be utterly worthless.

Note II.

DIMENSIONS OF REDOUBTS.

THE dimension of a square redoubt is determined by the condition of finding a terreplein large enough for the accommodation of its garrison, 15 square feet being allowed at the bivouac for every man.

The interior slope, banquette, and slope of banquette occupying 24 feet, it follows that a redoubt of 24 feet faces would have no terreplein, and could not be garrisoned.

FIG. 229.

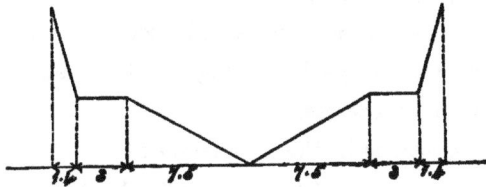

The smallest possible redoubt is found by the following calculation :—

Let x be the length of its side expressed in feet, and N the number of men destined to defend the work. The surface of the terreplein is $(x-24)^2$; the space required by the men is $15\,N$; therefore $(x-24)^2 = 15\,N$; and in supposing one man per lineal yard of the parapet, $N = \dfrac{4\,x}{3}$.

In resolving these equations, we find $x = 58$, $N = 77$. Thus the smallest possible redoubt would have a side of 58 feet and a garrison of 77 men.

In enclosed works the opening left for the ingress and egress of the garrison is masked by a traverse occupying about 500 square feet of the terreplein; the above equations should therefore be:

$$(x - 24)^2 - 500 = 15 \ N.$$
$$\frac{4\,x}{3} = N,$$

giving a side of 67 feet and a garrison of 89 men.

In the above cases, the whole terreplein is occupied, and, as we have said, there is not even room left for the fall of a shell !

It is necessary to calculate the minimum of a redoubt on more rational conditions. With a man only per lineal yard of the parapet, the defence would soon become slack, on account of the losses. A reserve is indispensable. Two-thirds of the garrison are on the banquette, one-third stands on the terreplein, forming the reserve.

The equations in this case become—

$$(x - 24)^2 - 500 = 15 \ N.$$
$$2 \ x = N.$$

Giving $x = 77$ feet, $N = 154$ men.

If the defenders are disposed in two ranks, the banquette must be enlarged to 4 feet 6 inches, and the space occupied by the slopes becomes 27 feet.

With two men per lineal yard of parapet, the equations are

$$(x - 27)^2 - 500 = 15 \ N.$$
$$4 \ x = N.$$

Hence $x = 112$ feet, $N = 418$.

In the same manner the minima would be calculated for three men per yard, &c.

In taking for granted that a man when in file occupies $2\frac{1}{4}$ square feet, the annexed table (p. 214) results from the calculations referred to:

When artillery is employed, every piece with its accessaries requires about 400 square feet of terreplein, and every platform with its ramp about 500.

The interior surface left for the garrison is therefore, with a gun, $(x - 27)^2 - 400 - 500 - 500$; with two guns $(x - 27)^2 - 800 - 1000 - 500$; &c.

A gun along a face occupies 15 lineal feet of parapet, and about 40 feet when in capital.

Number of men per yard of parapet	Minima of the sides (in yards).	Garrison.			Surface of terreplein.*	Garrison in battle order.		Reserve only formed in battle.	
		Whole.	On the banquette.	Reserve.		Space occupied.	Space free.	Space occupied.	Space free.
					Sq. yds.				
1	25·6	154	103	51	255	39	216	13	242
1½	32·3	291	194	97	492	73	419	24	468
2	37·3	448	299	139	746	112	634	35	711
3	47·3	852	568	284	1412	213	1199	71	1341

* The surface occupied by the traverse has been subtracted therefrom.

NOTE III.

CALCULATION OF THE EQUALITY OF DEBLAI
AND REMBLAI.

In Field Fortification it is very important, in order to save both time and labour, that the earth extracted from the ditch should be in sufficient quantity to construct the parapet and its slopes, and that there should be no excess to remove.

As the workmen have no other tools than the shovel, this equality between the deblai and the remblai is necessary for every part of the intrenchment

Supposing the covering mass and the ditch to be of the same length, it is clear that their volume would be equal if their profiles were of equal surface. The problem to solve, knowing the surface of the profile of the covering mass, consists in giving to the ditch such depth and width as to make the surface of its profile equal to that of the remblai.

But when earth is excavated it increases in bulk, and whatever care be taken in ramming it in, the volume it occupies in the remblai will be greater than the space it filled in the deblai. This increase of bulk, $\frac{1}{f}$ called in French *foisonnement*, is $\frac{1}{8}$th in strong soil, $\frac{1}{13}$th in ordinary soil, and $\frac{1}{10}$th in sand ; and it is indispensable to take it into account.

Let S, the surface of the profile of the remblai, be calculated by decomposing it into triangles and trapeziums,* that of the deblai S' will be found by the relation

$$S' + \frac{S'}{f} = S \qquad S' = S\frac{(f)}{(f+1)}$$

The depth D being assumed, the slopes of escarp and counterscarp being also known from the nature of the soil (page 18), the

---

* The surface of a long square is equal to the product of two adjacent sides. If $bc = 4$ yards, and $ab = 2$ yards, the surface, $4 \times 2 = 8$ square yards.

The surface of a triangle is equal to its base multiplied by half its altitude. If $AB = 3$ yards, and $CD = 4$ yards, the surface $= 3 \times 2$, or 6 square yards.

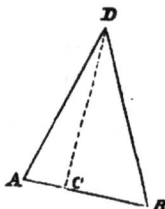

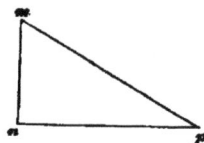

If $mn = 2$, $np = 3$, the surface $= 1 \times 3$, or 3 square yards.

The surface of a trapezium is equal to half the sum of its parallel sides, multiplied by its altitude.

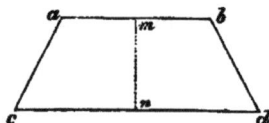

If $ab = 5$ yards, and $cd = 8$ yards, and $mn = 3$ yards, the surface $= \frac{(5+8)}{2} \times 3 = 19\cdot5$ square yards.

only dimension to ascertain is the width, x, of the bottom.

Calling $\frac{1}{t}$ the slope of escarp, $\frac{1}{t'}$ that of counterscarp, the sur-

face of the triangles shaded is $\frac{D^2}{2t} + \frac{D^2}{2t'}$, that of the rectangle, Dx

therefore $\frac{D^2}{2t} + \frac{D^2}{2t'} + Dx = S'$. Equation of the first degree, from

which the value of x is easily found. Let us apply this to a

FIG. 230.

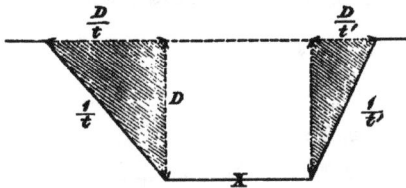

numerical example. The relief is 8 ft., the parapet 12 ft. thick, the foisonnement $\frac{1}{8}$th; the slope of scarp $\frac{2}{3}$; that of counter-scarp $\frac{1}{2}$; the depth 9 ft. It is required to find the width of the ditch.

FIG. 231.

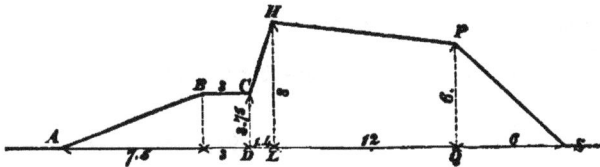

Trapezium $ABCD = \dfrac{(3+7\cdot5+3)}{2}3\cdot75 = 25\cdot31$ sq. ft.

Ditto . . $CDLH = \dfrac{(3\cdot75+8)}{2}$ $1\cdot43 = 8\cdot22$ sq. ft.

Ditto . . $HLPQ = \dfrac{(8+6)}{2}$ $12 = 84$ sq. ft.

Triangle . $PQS = \dfrac{(6+6)}{2}$ $= 18$ sq. ft.

———————   ———————

S $= 135\cdot53$ sq. ft.

Therefore the surface of the profile of the ditch will be

$$\frac{8}{9}S = 120\cdot47.$$

Fig. 232.

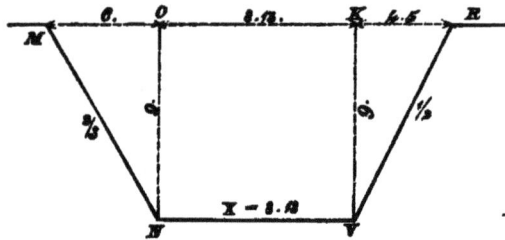

Now in the triangle MON, the side $MO = \frac{2}{3} ON = 6$; there-fore the area $= \dfrac{6\times9}{2} = 27$ sq. ft.; in triangle KVR, $KR = \frac{1}{2}KV = 4\cdot5$, hence the area $= \dfrac{4\cdot5\times9}{2} = 20\cdot25$. Besides, rectangle $OKNV = 9x$, therefore the total surface $= 27 + 20\cdot25 + 9x$, or $47\cdot25 + 9x$, it must measure $120\cdot47$. Hence the equation, $47\cdot25 + 9x = 120\cdot47$, giving $x = 8\cdot13$ width at the bottom. With this we find the width at the top, and every dimension is known.

In intrenchments presenting a series of salient and re-entering angles, the deblai and remblai are not of the same length. In overlooking the difference, there will be excess at the salients (1), and deficiency at the corners (2), the former being far greater than the latter. The surplus of earth should then be employed to construct a bonnette or a glacis.

Fig. 233.

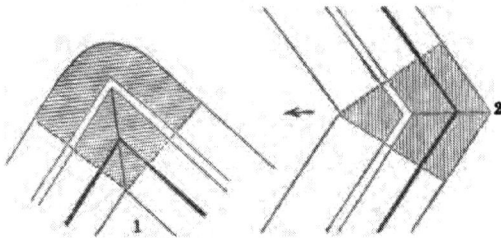

There are methods of calculating exactly the volume of excavation, but they cannot find place here; and the method above noticed will be found sufficiently approximative for field purposes.

Should the work be defiladed, and its relief increased at the salients, several profiles should be made, their areas calculated, and a mean surface adopted to find a mean profile for the ditch.

In that case the workmen should, whilst excavating, throw the earth obliquely towards the salients, to make up for the increase of relief thereon.

Note IV.

As we have said, it is not always possible in the field to throw up works with accuracy; the chief of a detachment, upon receiving news of the arrival of the enemy, cannot waste time in calculations, but he sets his men to work at once, and makes them excavate a trench that will give a cover, which, time permitting, is afterwards converted into a regular breastwork. Tools may be wanting; then recourse is had to such accidents as the ground may present. It would require volumes to enter into the never-ending details of the peculiar circumstances in which the vicissitudes of war may place an officer. If he is well acquainted with the spirit of fortification, it matters but little if he cannot recollect all the figures and dimensions given above; his sagacity will suggest what is best to be done. It is needless to tell him that if he has to defend a village against an enemy having artillery, he must remove the thatch from the roofs, barricade the streets, &c. &c.

A mere wall will become a good cover for him.

Fig. 234.

A hedge, with little trouble, will be transformed into a breastwork.

Fig. 235.

The banks of a river, when ever so little inclined, will soon become a good position.

The slope of a hill, by merely cutting down the inequalities it presents (an operation called *scarping*), will render his position difficult of access.

Fig. 236.

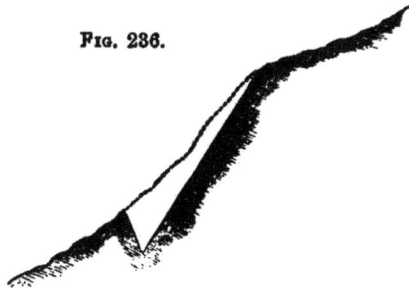

P

The more we investigate this subject, the more convinced we become that military history is the best complement of all military sciences.   There, indeed, we see that *much* can be done with *little*.

In India, sun-dried bricks, mud, and even tiers of camel saddles, have served to construct intrenchments.   At Paris, paving stones have answered the same purpose.   At the attack of Edinburgh (1688), at Fort San Christoval (1810), at Bhurtpoor (1825), in America, &c., cotton bales and woolpacks have proved of great advantage.   At Lisbon (1810), scarping was employed on a large scale.   At San Sebastian (1812), a redoubt was erected with casks to support the trenches of attack on the isthmus.   At Badajoz, sword-blades, transformed into chevaux-de-frise, became an insurmountable obstacle, &c. &c.

THE END.

LONDON :
SAVILL AND EDWARDS, PRINTERS, CHANDOS STREET,
COVENT GARDEN.

STANDARD BOOKS

PUBLISHED BY

JOHN W. PARKER AND SON, WEST STRAND.

The Kingdom and People of Siam.
By Sir JOHN BOWRING, F.R.S., Her Majesty's Plenipotentiary in China. Two Vols. With Map and Illustrations. 32s.

History of Normandy and of England. By Sir F. PALGRAVE. Vols. I. and II. 21s. each.

The Spanish Conquest in America, and its Relation to the History of Slavery and to the Government of Colonies. By ARTHUR HELPS. Vols. I. and II. 28s. Vol. III. 16s.

History of the Inductive Sciences. By W. WHEWELL, D.D., Master of Trinity College, Cambridge. Cheaper Edition, Three Vols., small 8vo.

Biographical History of Philosophy. By G. H. LEWES. Library Edition. Octavo. Thoroughly Revised and greatly Enlarged. 16s.

State Papers and Correspondence, illustrative of the Political and Social State of Europe, from the Revolution to the Accession of the House of Hanover. With Historical Introduction, Memoirs, and Notes, by J. M. KEMBLE, M.A. 16s.

Bacon's Essays. With Annotations. By RICHARD WHATELY, D.D., Archbishop of Dublin. Third Edit. Octavo. 10s. 6d.

Principles and Maxims of Jurisprudence. By J. G. PHILLIMORE, Q.C. 12s.

History of England, from the Fall of Wolsey to the Death of Elizabeth. By J. A. FROUDE, M.A., late Fellow of Exeter College, Oxford. Vols. I. and II. Octavo. 26s.

History of England during the Reign of George the Third. By W. MASSEY, M.P. Vol. I. 12s.

Oxford Essays. 1855, 1856, 1857. 7s. 6d. each.

Cambridge Essays. 1855, 1856. 7s. 6d. each.

Suggestions for the Repression of Crime. By M. D. HILL, Q.C. 16s.

Friends in Council. New Edition. Two Vols. 9s.

Companions of my Solitude. New Edition. 3s. 6d.

Tour in the Principalities, Crimea, and Countries adjacent to the Black Sea, in 1835-6. By Lord DE ROS. 4s. 6d.

The Gospel according to St. John after the Authorised Version. Newly compared with the Original Greek, and revised by—
JOHN BARROW, D.D.
GEORGE MOBERLY, D.C.L.
HENRY ALFORD, B.D.
WILLIAM G. HUMPHRY, B.D.
CHARLES J. ELLICOTT, M.A. 2s. 6d.

Annotated Edition of the English Poets. By ROBERT BELL. In volumes. 2s. 6d., in cloth.

Chaucer. Eight Volumes. 20s.

Thomson. Two Volumes. 5s.

Shakspeare's Poems. 2s. 6d.

Butler. Three Volumes. 7s. 6d.

Dryden. Three Volumes. 7s. 6d.

Cowper. With Selections from Lloyd, Cotton, Brooke, Darwin, and Hayley. Three Volumes. 7s. 6d.

Surrey, Minor Contemporaneous Poets, and Lord Buckhurst. 2s. 6d.

Songs from the Dramatists. 2s. 6d.

Sir Thomas Wyatt. 2s. 6d.

John Oldham. 2s. 6d.

Edmund Waller. 2s. 6d.

Ben Jonson. 2s. 6d.

Early Ballads. 2s. 6d.

Greene and Marlowe, 2s. 6d.

Ancient Poems, Ballads, and Songs of the Peasantry. 2s. 6d.

Letters from the United States, Cuba, and Canada. By the Hon. AMELIA M. MURRAY. Two Volumes. 16s.

The Senses and the Intellect. By ALEX. BAIN, M.A. Octavo. 15s.

Of the Plurality of Worlds: an Essay. Fourth Edition. 6s.

The Mediterranean: a Memoir, Physical, Historical, and Nautical. By Admiral SMYTH. 15s.

Cloister Life of Charles the Fifth. By W. STIRLING, M.P. Third Edition. 8s.

Velazquez and his Works. By W. STIRLING, M.P. 6s.

Modern Painting at Naples. By LORD NAPIER. 4s. 6d.

Principles of Political Economy. By J. STUART MILL. Fourth Edition. Two Volumes. Octavo. 30s.

System of Logic. By the same. Cheaper Edition. Two Volumes. 25s.

Goethe's Opinions on Mankind, Literature, Science, and Art. 3s. 6d.

The Roman Empire of the West. By R. CONGREVE, M.A. 4s.

On the Credibility of the Early Roman History. By the Right Hon. Sir G. C. LEWIS, Bart., M.P. Two Vols. 30s.

On the Methods of Observation and Reasoning in Politics. By the Rt. Hon. Sir G. C. LEWIS, Bart., M.P. Two Vols. 28s.

On the Influence of Authority in Matters of Opinion. By the same. 10s. 6d.

History of the Whig Ministry of 1830, to the passing of the Reform Bill. By J. A. ROEBUCK, M.P. Two Vols. 28s.

History of Trial by Jury. By W. FORSYTH, M.A. Octavo. 8s. 6d.

Introductory Lectures on Political Economy. By R. WHATELY, D.D., Archbishop of Dublin. Fourth Edition. 8s.

The Institutes of Justinian; with English Introduction, Translation, and Notes. By T. C. SANDARS, M.A. 15s.

Varronianus; a Critical and Historical Introduction to the Study of the Latin Language. By J. W. DONALDSON, D.D. Second Edition. 14s.

The New Cratylus; Contributions towards a more accurate Knowledge of the Greek Language. By Dr. DONALDSON. Second Edition, enlarged. 18s.

Ancient and Modern Fish Tattle. By the Rev. C. D. BADHAM, M.D. 12s.

Leaves from the Note-Book of a Naturalist. By W. J. BRODERIP, F.R.S. 10s. 6d.

Discourse on the Studies of the University of Cambridge. By Professor SEDGWICK, M.A. Fifth Edition, 12s.

Lectures on Education, delivered at the Royal Institution of Great Britain. 6s.

Elements of Logic. By R. WHATELY, D.D., Archbishop of Dublin. 4s. 6d. Octavo, 10s. 6d.

Elements of Rhetoric. By the same Author. 4s. 6d. Octavo, 10s. 6d.

Philosophy of the Inductive Sciences. By Dr. WHEWELL. Second Edition. Two Volumes. Octavo. 30s.

Indications of the Creator—Extracts from Dr. WHEWELL's History and Philosophy of Inductive Sciences. 5s. 6d.

Atlas of Physical and Historical Geography. Engraved by J. W. LOWRY. 5s.

Elements of Morality. By Dr. WHEWELL. Third Edition. Two Vols. 15s.

Manual of Geographical Science. PART THE FIRST, 10s. 6d., containing—
MATHEMATICAL GEOGRAPHY. By Rev. M. O'BRIEN.
PHYSICAL GEOGRAPHY. By T. D. ANSTED, M.A., F.R.S.
CHARTOGRAPHY. By J. R. JACKSON, F.R.S.
GEOGRAPHICAL TERMINOLOGY. By Rev. C. G. NICOLAY.

Lectures on History of Moral Philosophy in England. By Dr. WHEWELL. 8s.

Lectures on Systematic Morality. By Dr. WHEWELL. 7s. 6d.

History of the Royal Society, compiled from Original Authentic Documents. By C. R. WELD. Two Volumes. 30s.

The Comets. By J. RUSSELL HIND. 5s. 6d.

An Astronomical Vocabulary. By the same Author. 1s. 6d.

Cycle of Celestial Objects. By Admiral W. H. SMYTH. Two Vols. With Illustrations. £2 2s.

Elements of Chemistry. By W. A. MILLER, M.D., F.R.S., Professor of Chemistry, King's College. Complete in Three Parts. £2 6s. 6d.

First Lines in Chemistry. By A. J. BERNAYS. With 179 Illustrations. 7s.

Manual of Chemistry. By W. T. BRANDE, F.R.S. Sixth Edition, much enlarged. Two large volumes. £2 5s.

Dictionary of Materia Medica and Pharmacy. By the same Author. 15s.

Principles of Mechanism. By Professor WILLIS, M.A., F.R.S.

Lectures on Astronomy. By H. MOSELEY, M.A., F.R.S. Cheaper Edition, revised. 3s. 6d.

Elements of Meteorology. By the late Professor DANIELL. With Plates. Two Volumes. Octavo. 32s.

On Thunder Storms, and on the Means of Protecting Buildings and Shipping against the Effects of Lightning. By Sir W. SNOW HARRIS, F.R.S. 10s. 6d.

Connexion of Natural and Divine Truth. By BADEN POWELL, M.A., F.R.S., Professor of Geometry, Oxford. 9s.

Undulatory Theory as applied to the Dispersion of Light. By the same. 9s.

Structure and Functions of the Human Spleen. By H. GRAY, F.R.S. With 64 Illustrations. 15s.

Lectures on the Principles and Practice of Physic. By THOMAS WATSON, M.D. Fourth Edition, revised. Two Volumes. Octavo.

On the Diseases of the Kidney. By GEORGE JOHNSON, M.D., Physician to King's College Hospital. 14s.

On Epidemic Diarrhœa and Cholera; their Pathology and Treatment. With a Record of Cases. By the same. 7s. 6d.

Sanitary Condition of the City of London (from 1848 to 1853). With Preface and Notes. By JOHN SIMON, F.R.S. 8s. 6d.

Physiological Anatomy and Physiology of Man. By Dr. TODD, F.R.S., and W. BOWMAN, F.R.S. Complete in Two Volumes. £2.

On Medical Evidence and Testimony in Cases of Lunacy. By T. MAYO, M.D., F.R.S. 3s. 6d.

The Philosophy of Living. By HERBERT MAYO, M.D. Cheaper Edition. 5s.

Management of the Organs of Digestion. By the same. 6s. 6d.

Lunacy and Lunatic Life. 3s. 6d.

German Mineral Waters: and their Employment for the Cure of certain Chronic Diseases. By S. SUTRO, M.D. 7s. 6d.

Spasm, Languor, and Palsy. By J. A. WILSON, M.D. 7s.

Gout, Chronic Rheumatism, and Inflammation of the Joints. By R. B. TODD, M.D., F.R.S. 7s. 6d.

Minerals and their Uses. By J. R. JACKSON, F.R.S. With Frontispiece. 7s. 6d.

Lectures on Dental Physiology and Surgery. By J. TOMES, F.R.S. Octavo. With 100 Illustrations. 12s.

Use and Management of Artificial Teeth. By the same Author. 3s. 6d.

Practical Chemistry for Farmers and Landowners. By J. TRIMMER, F.G.S. 5s.

Practical Geodesy. By BUTLER WILLIAMS, C.E. 8s. 6d.

Manual for Teaching Model-Drawing. By the same. 15s.

Instructions in Drawing. Abridged from the above. 3s.

Chemistry of the Four Ancient Elements. By T. GRIFFITHS. 4s. 6d.

Recreations in Chemistry. By the same. Second Edition, enlarged. 5s.

Recreations in Astronomy. By Rev. L. TOMLINSON, M.A. Third Edition. 4s. 6d.

Recreations in Physical Geography. By Miss R. M. ZORNLIN. Fifth Edition. 6s.

World of Waters; or, Recreations in Hydrology. By the same Author. 4s. 6d.

Recreations in Geology. By the same Author. Third Edition. 4s. 6d.

Elements of Fortification, for the Use of Students, Civilian and Military. By CAPTAIN LENDY. With numerous Woodcuts.

Guyot's Earth and Man. Cheap Edition. 2s.

Shipwrecks of the Royal Navy. By W. O. S. GILLY. With Preface by Dr. GILLY. 7s. 6d.

Danger of Superficial Knowledge. By Professor J. D. FORBES. 2s.

Meliora; or, Better Times to Come. Edited by Viscount INGESTRE, M.P. Two Series. 5s. each.

Introductory Lectures delivered at Queen's College, London. 5s.

Days and Hours. By FREDERICK TENNYSON. 6s.

The Angel in the House. Complete in Two Parts. 12s.

The Saint's Tragedy. By C. KINGSLEY, Rector of Eversley. Cheaper Edition. 2s.

Justin Martyr, and other Poems. By R. C. TRENCH. Fourth Edition. 6s.

Poems from Eastern Sources: Genoveva and other Poems. By the same. 5s. 6d.

Elegiac Poems. By the same. 2s. 6d.

The Poems of Goethe. Translated by EDGAR A. BOWRING. 7s. 6d.

Schiller's Poems, Complete. Translated by EDGAR ALFRED BOWRING. 6s.

Calderon's Life's a Dream: the Great Theatre of the World. With an Essay on his Life and Genius, by R. CHENEVIX TRENCH. 4s. 6d.

Six Dramas of Calderon. Translated by EDWARD FITZGERALD. 4s. 6d.

Dynevor Terrace. By the Author of The Heir of Redclyffe. Two Vols. 12s.

Still Waters. By the Author of Dorothy. Two Volumes. 9s.

The Daisy Chain. By the Author of The Heir of Redclyffe. Two Vols. 10s. 6d.

The Lances of Lynwood. By the same Author. Cheap Edition. 3s.

Kate Coventry, an Autobiography. By the Author of Digby Grand. 7s. 6d.

Digby Grand. By Major WHYTE MELVILLE. Cheap Edition. 5s.

General Bounce. By Major WHYTE MELVILLE. Two Volumes. 15s.

The Myrtle and the Heather. By the Author of Gwen. Two Volumes. 9s.

Gwen; or, the Cousins. By A. M. GOODRICH. Two Volumes. 9s.

Heartsease. By the Author of The Heir of Redclyffe. Cheap Edition. 6s.

Heir of Redclyffe. Cheap Edition. 6s.

The Wedding Guests; or, the Happiness of Life. By MARY C. HUME. Two Volumes. Post Octavo. 16s.

Light and Shade; or, the Young Artist. By ANNA H. DRURY. 6s.

Friends and Fortune. By ANNA H. DRURY. Second Edition. 6s.

The Inn by the Sea-Side. By ANNA H. DRURY. An Allegory. 2s.

Yeast: a Problem. By C. KINGSLEY, Rector of Eversley. Cheaper Edition. 5s.

Hypatia. By C. KINGSLEY. Cheaper Edition. One Volume. 6s.

Compensation. A Story of Real Life Thirty Years Ago. Two Volumes. 9s.

Dorothy. A Tale. 4s. 6d.

De Cressy. A Tale. By the Author of 'Dorothy.' 4s. 6d.

The Upper Ten Thousand: Sketches of American Society. By A NEW YORKER. 5s.

Clara Morison: A Tale of South Australia during the Gold Fever. Two Volumes. 9s.

The Youth and Womanhood of Helen Tyrrel. By the Author of Brampton Rectory. 6s.

Brampton Rectory; or, the Lesson of Life. Second Edition. 8s. 6d.

Compton Merivale. By the Author of Brampton Rectory. 8s. 6d.

The Cardinal Virtues. By HARRIETTE CAMPBELL. Two Volumes. 7s.

The Merchant and the Friar. By Sir F. PALGRAVE. Second Edition. 3s.

The Little Duke. By the Author of Heartsease. Cheap Edition. 1s. 6d.

The Crusaders. By T. KEIGHTLEY. 7s.

The Lord and the Vassal; a Familiar Exposition of the Feudal System. 2s.

French Revolution; its Causes and Consequences. By F. M. ROWAN. 3s. 6d.

Labaume's History of Napoleon's Invasion of Russia. 2s. 6d.

Historical Sketch of the British Army. By G. R. GLEIG, M.A. 3s. 6d.

Family History of England. By the same. Three Volumes. 10s. 6d.

Familiar History of Birds. By E. STANLEY, D.D., Bishop of Norwich. Seventh Edition. 3s. 6d.

Domesticated Animals. By MARY ROBERTS. Cheaper Edition. 2s. 6d.

Wild Animals. By the same. 2s. 6d.

Young Officer's Companion. By LORD DE ROS. Cheaper Edition. 6s.

Popular Physiology. By P. B. LORD, M.B. Cheaper Edition, revised. 5s.

Amusements in Chess. By C. TOMLINSON. 4s. 6d.

Musical History, Biography, and Criticism. By GEORGE HOGARTH. Two Volumes. 10s. 6d.

Chronicles of the Seasons. In Four Books, 3s. 6d. each.

Ullmann's Gregory of Nazianzum. A Contribution to the Ecclesiastical History of the Fourth Century. Translated by G. V. COX, M.A. 6s.

Neander's Julian the Apostate and his Generation: an Historical Picture. Translated by G. V. COX, M.A. 3s. 6d.

Dahlmann's Life of Herodotus. Translated by G. V. COX, M.A. 5s.

Student's Manual of Ancient History. By W. COOKE TAYLOR, LL.D. Cheaper Edition. 6s.

Student's Manual of Modern History. By the same. Cheaper Edition. 6s.

History of Mohammedanism. Cheaper Edition. By the same Author. 4s.

History of Christianity. By the same Author. 6s. 6d.

Hellas: the Home, History, Literature, and Arts of the Ancient Greeks. By F. JACOBS. Translated by J. OXENFORD. 4s. 6d.

Analysis of Grecian History. By DAWSON W. TURNER, M.A. 2s.

Analysis of Roman History. By the same Author. Second Edition. 2s.

Analysis of English and of French History. By the same. Third Edition. 2s.

Claudius Ptolemy and the Nile; or, an Inquiry into that Geographer's merit and errors, and the authenticity of the Mountains of the Moon. By W. D. COOLEY. With a Map. 4s.

The Holy City. By G. WILLIAMS, B.D. Second Edition, with Illustrations and Additions, and a Plan of Jerusalem. Two Vols. £2 5s.

History of the Holy Sepulchre. By PROFESSOR WILLIS. With Illustrations. 9s.

Plan of Jerusalem, from the Ordnance Survey. With a Memoir. Reprinted from Williams's Holy City. 9s.

Three Weeks in Palestine and Lebanon. Cheaper Edition. 2s.

Notes on German Churches. By Dr. WHEWELL. Third Edition. 12s.

View of the Art of Colonization. By E. GIBBON WAKEFIELD. Octavo. 12s.

On the Union of the Dominions of Great Britain, by Inter-communication with the Pacific and the East. By CAPTAIN M. H. SYNGE, R.E. With Maps. 8s. 6d.

A Year with the Turks. By WARINGTON W. SMYTH, M.A. 8s.

Gazpacho; or, Summer Months in Spain. By W. G. CLARK, M.A., Fellow of Trinity Coll. Camb. Cheaper Edition. 5s.

Auvergne, Piedmont, and Savoy; a Summer Ramble. By C. R. WELD. 8s. 6d.

Wanderings in the Republics of Western America. By G. BYAM. 7s. 6d.

Lectures on the Characters of our Lord's Apostles. 3s. 6d.

Lectures on the Scripture Revelations respecting good and Evil Angels. By the same Author. 3s. 6d.

View of the Scripture Revelations respecting a Future State. Seventh Edition. By the same Author. 5s.

Sermons, Preached and Published on several occasions. By SAMUEL, Lord Bishop of Oxford. Octavo. 10s. 6d.

Six Sermons preached before the University. By the Bishop of Oxford. 4s. 6d.

The Greek Testament. With Notes, Grammatical and Exegetical. By W. WEBSTER, M.A., of King's College, London, and W. F. WILKINSON, M.A., Vicar of St. Werburgh, Derby. Vol. I. containing the Gospels and Acts of the Apostles. 20s.

Thoughts for the Holy Week. By the Author of Amy Herbert.

The Catechist's Manual; being a Series of Readings from St. Mark's Gospel. By Bishop HINDS. Second Edition. 4s. 6d.

History and Theology of the Three Creeds. By W. WIGAN HARVEY, M.A., Rector of Buckland. Two Volumes. 14s.

Sermons for the Times. By C. KINGSLEY, Rector of Eversley. 5s.

Twenty-five Village Sermons. By C. KINGSLEY. Cheap Edition. 2s. 6d.

Churchman's Theological Dictionary. By R. EDEN, M.A. Second Edition. 5s.

The Gospel Narrative according to the Authorized Text. With Marginal Proofs and Notes. By J. FORSTER, M.A. Fourth Edition. 12s.

Statutes relating to the Ecclesiastical and Eleemosynary Institutions of England, Wales, Ireland, India, and the Colonies; with Decisions. By A. J. STEPHENS, M.A. F.R.S. Two Volumes, with Indices. £3 3s.

Historical and Explanatory Treatise on the Book of Common Prayer. By W. G. HUMPHRY, B.D., 7s. 6d.

Scripture Female Characters. By the VISCOUNTESS HOOD. 3s. 6d.

The Natural History of Infidelity and Superstition in Contrast with Christian Faith. Bampton Lectures. By J. E. RIDDLE, M.A. Octavo. 12s.

Manual of Christian Antiquities. By the same Author. Second Edition. 18s.

Luther and his Times. By the same. 5s.

Churchman's Guide to the Use of the English Liturgy. By the same. 3s. 6d.

First Sundays at Church. By the same Author. Cheaper Edition. 2s. 6d.

Introduction to the Study of the Old Testament. By A. BARRY, M.A., Head Master of Leeds Gram. School. Part I. 6s.

Exposition of the Thirty-nine Articles. By E. HAROLD BROWNE, M.A., Norrisian Professor of Divinity, Cambridge. Cheaper Edition. One Volume. 16s.

Examination Questions on Professor Browne's Exposition of the Articles. By J. GORLE, M.A.

The Churchman's Guide; an Index of Sermons and other Works, arranged according to their Subjects. By JOHN FORSTER, M.A. Octavo. 7s.

The Early Christians. By W. PRIDDEN, M.A. Cheaper Edition. 2s. 6d.

The Book of the Fathers, and the Spirit of their Writings. 9s. 6d.

Babylon and Jerusalem: a Letter to Countess of Hahn-Hahn. 2s. 6d.

History of the Church of England. By T. VOWLER SHORT, D.D., Lord Bishop of St. Asaph. Cheaper Edition. 10s. 6d.

Burnet's History of the Reformation, abridged. Edited by Dr. CORRIE, Master of Jesus College, Cambridge. 10s. 6d.

History of the English Reformation. By F. C. MASSINGBERD, M.A. Third Edition, enlarged. 6s.

History of Popery. 9s. 6d.

Elizabethan Religious History. By H. SOAMES, M.A. Octavo. 16s.

The Anglo-Saxon Church; its History, Revenues, and General Character. By H. SOAMES, M.A. Cheaper Edition. 7s. 6d.

History of the Christian Church. By Dr. Burton, Professor of Divinity, Oxford. 5s.

Outlines of Sacred History. 2s. 6d.

Outlines of Ecclesiastical History; Before the Reformation. By the Rev. W. H. Hoare, M.A. 2s. 6d.

Bible Maps; with copious Index. By W. Hughes. Coloured. 5s.

The Three Treacherous Dealers: An Illustration of the Church Catechism. By J. W. Donaldson, D.D. 2s. 6d.

Civil History of the Jews. By O. Cockayne, M.A., King's College. 4s. 6d.

Cudworth on Freewill. Edited, with Notes, by Archdeacon Allen, 3s.

Guericke's Manual of the Antiquities of the Christian Church. Translated by the Rev. A. J. W. Morrison. 5s. 6d.

Garrick's Mode of Reading the Liturgy. With Notes, and a Discourse on Public Reading. By R. Cull. 5s. 6d.

The Four Gospels in one Narrative. Arranged by Two Friends. 4s. 6d.

Life of Mrs. Godolphin. By John Evelyn. Edited by the Bishop of Oxford. Third Edition, with Portrait. 6s.

Remains of Bishop Copleston. With Reminiscences of his Life. By the Archbishop of Dublin. With Portrait. 10s. 6d.

Memoir of Bishop Copleston. By W. J. Copleston, M.A. 10s. 6d.

Life of Archbishop Usher. By C. R. Elrington, D.D. Portrait. 12s.

Life of Archbishop Sancroft. By Dr. D'Oyly. Octavo. 9s.

Memoirs of Bishop Butler. By T. Bartlett, M.A. 12s.

Lives of Eminent Christians. By R. B. Hone, M.A., Archdeacon of Worcester. Four Volumes. 18s.

Bishop Jeremy Taylor; His Predecessors, Contemporaries, and Successors. By Rev. R. A. Willmott. 5s.

Lives of English Sacred Poets. By the same Author. Two Vols. 9s.

Life and Services of Lord Harris. By the Right Hon. S. R. Lushington. Second Edition. 6s. 6d.

Bacon's Essays; with the Colours of Good and Evil. With the References and Notes. By T. Markby, M.A. 1s. 6d.

Bacon's Advancement of Learning. Revised, with References and Notes, and an Index. By T. Markby, M.A. 2s.

Principles of Imitative Art. By George Butler, M.A. 6s.

Butler's Sermons on Human Nature. With Preface by Dr. Whewell. 3s. 6d.

Butler's Sermons on Moral Subjects. With Preface by Dr. Whewell. 3s. 6d.

Notes on the Parables. By R. Chenevix Trench, D.D., Dean of Westminster. Sixth Edition. 12s.

Notes on the Miracles. By the same Author. Fifth Edition. 12s.

Five Sermons preached before the University of Cambridge in November, 1856. By the same Author. 2s. 6d.

Hulsean Lectures. By the same Author. Cheaper Edition. 5s.

St. Augustine's Exposition of the Sermon on the Mount. With an Essay on St. Augustine as an Interpreter of Scripture. By R. C. Trench, D.D. Second Edition. 7s. The Essay separately, 3s. 6d.

Literature of the Church of England; Specimens of the Writings of Eminent Divines, with Memoirs of their Lives and Times. By R. Cattermole, B.D. Two volumes. Octavo. 25s.

Essays on Peculiarities of the Christian Religion. By R. Whately, D.D., Archbishop of Dublin. Cheaper Edition. 7s. 6d.

Essays on Difficulties in the Writings of the Apostle Paul. By the same Author. Cheaper Edition. 8s.

Essays on Errors of Romanism. By the same. Cheaper Edition. 7s. 6d.

Essays on Dangers to Christian Faith from the Teaching or the Conduct of its Professors. By the same Author. 10s.

The Scripture Doctrine concerning the Sacraments. By the same. 2s. 6d.

Cautions for the Times. Edited by the Archbishop of Dublin. 7s.

English Synonyms. Edited by Archbishop of Dublin. Third Edition. 3s.

Synonyms of the New Testament. By R. Chenevix Trench, D.D. Dean of Westminster. Third Edition. 5s.

English, Past and Present. By the same Author. Third Edition, enlarged. 4s.

On the Lessons in Proverbs. By the same Author. Third Edition. 3s.

On the Study of Words. By the same Author. Seventh Edition. 3s. 6d.

Sacred Latin Poetry. With Notes and Introduction. By the same. 7s.

Dialogues on Divine Providence.
By a Fellow of a College. 3s. 6d.

The Church, its Nature and Offices.
By C. P. Reichel, B.D., Professor of Latin
in the Queen's University. 6s.

Liber Precum Publicarum; Ordo
Administrandæ Cœnæ Domini, Catechismus, Ecclesiæ Anglicanæ. Psalterium.
5s. 6d. cloth; 10s. 6d. calf.

Sequentiæ ex Missalibus, Anglicis,
Gallicis, Germanicis Desumptæ. Collegit,
notulasque addidit J. M. Neale, A.M. 7s.

Ordo Sæclorum; a Treatise on the
Chronology of the Holy Scriptures. By
H. Browne, M.A., Canon of Chichester. 20s.

Pearson on the Creed, revised and
corrected. By Temple Chevallier, B.D.
12s.

James on the Corruptions of Scripture, Councils, and Fathers, by the Prelates, Pastors, and Pillars of the Church of
Rome. Revised by J. E. Cox, M.A. 12s.

Fullwood's Roma Ruit. The Pillars
of Rome Broken. New Edition, by C.
Hardwick, M.A. Octavo. 10s. 6d.

College Lectures on Ecclesiastical
History. By W. Bates, B.D., Fellow of
Christ's College, Cambridge. 6s. 6d.

College Lectures on Christian Antiquities. By the same. 9s.

The True Faith of a Christian;
being a simple Exposition of the Apostles'
Creed. By Rev. C. J. D'Oyly. 2s. 6d.

Choral Service of the Church: an
Inquiry into the Liturgical System of the
Cathedral and Collegiate Foundations. By
J. Jebb, M.A., Rector of Peterstow. 16s.

The Personality of the Tempter.
By C. J. Vaughan, D.D., Head Master of
Harrow School. Octavo. 7s. 6d.

Sermons Preached in the Chapel of
Harrow School. By the same Author.
Second Series. 12s.

Sermons preached before the University of Oxford. By C. A. Ogilvie, D.D.,
Canon of Christ Church. Octavo. 5s.

Lectures on the Prophecies. By A.
M'Caul, D.D., Professor of Divinity in
King's College, London. Octavo. 7s.

The Messiahship of Jesus. By
Dr. M'Caul. 7s.

Discourses on Christian Humiliation
and on the City of God. By C. H. Terrot,
D.D., Bishop of Edinburgh. 7s. 6d.

College Chapel Sermons. By W.
Whewell, D.D. 10s. 6d.

Small Books on Great Subjects.

Philosophical Theories and Philosophical
Experience. 3s. 6d.
On the Connexion between Physiology and
Intellectual Science. 3s. 6d.
On Man's Power over Himself to prevent or
control Insanity. 3s. 6d.
Introduction to Practical Organic Chemistry.
3s. 6d.
Brief View of Greek Philosophy to the Age
of Pericles. 3s. 6d.
Greek Philosophy from Socrates to the
Coming of Christ. 3s. 6d.
Christian Doctrine and Practice in the
Second Century. 3s. 6d.
Exposition of Vulgar and Common Errors.
3s. 6d.
Introduction to Vegetable Physiology. 3s. 6d.
On the Principles of Criminal Law. 3s. 6d.
Christian Sects in the Nineteenth Century.
3s. 6d.
General Principles of Grammar. 3s. 6d.
Sketches of Geology. 3s. 6d.
State of Man before the Promulgation of
Christianity. 3s. 6d.
Thoughts and Opinions of a Statesman.
Second Edition. 3s. 6d.
On the Responsibilities of Employers. 3s. 6d.
Christian Doctrine and Practice in the Twelfth
Century. 3s. 6d.
The Philosophy of Ragged Schools. 3s. 6d.
On the State of Man subsequent to the Promulgation of Christianity. Four Parts.
4s. 6d. each.

CLASSICAL TEXTS, Carefully Revised.

Æschyli Eumenides. 1s.
Cæsar de Bello Gallico. I. to IV. 1s. 6d.
Cicero de Amicitia et de Senectute. 1s.
Cicero de Officiis. 2s.
Cicero pro Plancio. 1s.
Cicero pro Milone. 1s.
Cicero pro Muræna. 1s.
Ciceronis Oratio Philippica Secunda. 1s.
Demosthenes in Leptinem. 1s.
Demosthenes against Aphobus and
Onetor. 1s. 6d.
Euripidis Bacchæ. 1s.
Excerpta ex Arriano. 2s. 6d.
Excerpta ex Luciano. 2s. 6d.
Excerpta ex Taciti Annalibus. 2s. 6d.
Horatii Satiræ. 1s.
Horatii Carmina. 1s. 6d.
Horatii Ars Poetica. 6d.
Ovidii Fasti. 1s. 6d.
Platonis Phædo. 2s.
Platonis Menexenus. 1s.
Platonis Phædrus. 1s. 6d.
Plauti Miles Gloriosus. 1s.
Plauti Trinummus. 1s.
Plutarch's Lives of Solon, Pericles, and
Philopœmen. 2s.
Sophoclis Philoctetes, with Notes. 2s.
Sophoclis Œdipus Tyrannus, with Notes.
2s. 6d.
Taciti Germania. 1s.
Taciti Agricola. 1s.
Terentii Andria. 1s.
Terentii Adelphi. 1s.
Virgilii Georgica. 1s. 6d.

Notes upon Thucydides. Books I.
and II. By J. G. SHEPPARD, M.A., and
L. EVANS, M.A. 8s.

Platonis Philebus, with Notes by
C. BADHAM, D.D. 5s.

The Alcestis of Euripides; with Notes
by Bishop MONK. 4s. 6d.

Müller's Dissertations on the Eumenides of Æschylus. Cheaper Edition. 6s. 6d.

Propertius; with English Notes,
Preface on the State of Latin Scholarship,
and Indices. By F. A. PALEY. 10s. 6d.

Arundines Cami, sive Musarum Can-
tabrigiensium Lusus Canori, collegit atque
edidit HENRICUS DRURY, M.A. 12s.

Politics of Aristotle. With Notes.
By R. CONGREVE, M.A., Fellow and
Tutor of Wadham College, Oxford. 16s.

Choephoræ of Æschylus. With
Notes. By J. CONINGTON, M.A., Professor of Latin in the University of Oxford.

Agamemnon of Æschylus, the Text,
with a Translation into English Verse, and
Notes. By J. CONINGTON, M.A. 7s. 6d.

Æschylus translated into English
Verse. With Notes, and a Life of Æschylus.
By Professor BLACKIE. Two Volumes. 16s.

Phædrus, Lysis, and Protagoras of
Plato. Translated by J. WRIGHT, M.A.
4s. 6d.

Homeric Ballads: the Text, with
Metrical Translations and Notes. By the
late Dr. MAGINN. 6s.

Tacitus, the Complete Works, with
a Commentary, Life of Tacitus, Indices,
and Notes. Edited by Professor RITTER,
of Bonn. Four Volumes. Octavo. 28s.

Aristophanis Comœdiæ Vndecim,
cum Notis et Indice Historico, edidit
H. A. HOLDEN, A.M. Coll. Trin. Cant.
Socius. 15s. Plays separately, 1s. each.

Aulularia and Menæchemi of Plautus,
with Notes by J. HILDYARD, B.D., Fellow
of Christ's Coll., Camb. 7s. 6d. each.

Antigone of Sophocles, in Greek and
English, with Notes. By Dr. DONALD-
SON. 9s.

Pindar's Epinician Odes; with
copious Notes and Indices. By Dr.
DONALDSON. 16s.

Becker's Gallus; or, Roman Scenes
of the Time of Augustus, with Notes and
Excursus. Second Edition. 12s.

Becker's Charicles; or, Illustrations
of the Private Life of the Ancient Greeks.
Second Edition, carefully revised. 10s. 6d.

Speeches of Demosthenes against
Aphobus and Onetor. Translated, with
Notes, by C. RANN KENNEDY, M.A. 9s.

Greek Verses of Shrewsbury
School. By Dr. KENNEDY. 8s.

Select Private Orations of Demosthenes; with Notes. By C. T. PENROSE,
M.A. Cheaper Edition. 4s.

Frogs of Aristophanes; with English
Notes. By the Rev. H. P. COOKESLEY. 7s.

Classical Examination Papers of
King's College. By R. W. BROWNE, M.A.,
Professor of Classical Literature. 6s.

Longer Exercises in Latin Prose
Composition. By Dr. DONALDSON. 6s. 6d.

Manual of Latin Prose Composition.
By the Rev. H. MUSGRAVE WILKINS, M.A.,
Fellow of Merton College, Oxford, Author
of "Notes for Latin Lyrics." 4s. 6d.

Fables of Babrius. Edited by Sir
G. C. LEWIS, Bart., M.P. 5s. 6d.

Critical and Grammatical Commen-
tary on St. Paul's Epistles. By C. J.
ELLICOTT, M.A.
GALATIANS. 7s. 6d.
EPHESIANS. 7s. 6d.
THE PASTORAL EPISTLES 10s. 6d.

Commentary on the Acts of the
Apostles. By W. G. HUMPHRY, B.D.
Cheaper Edition, with a Map, 5s.

Pearson's Lectures on the Acts of
the Apostles and Annals of St. Paul.
Edited in English, with a few Notes, by
J. R. CROWFOOT, B.D. 4s.

Greek Text of the Acts of the
Apostles; with English Notes. By H.
ROBINSON, D.D. 8s.

Comparative Grammar of the Hebrew Language. By Dr. DONALDSON.
3s. 6d.

Hebrew Grammar. By CHR. LEO,
of Cambridge. 12s. 6d.

New Hebrew Lexicon. With Grammar, Vocabulary, &c. Also Chaldee Grammar and Lexicon. By T. JARRETT, M.A.,
Professor of Hebrew, Cambridge. 21s.

Phraseological and Explanatory
Notes on the Hebrew Text of the Book of
Genesis, by THEODORE PRESTON, M.A.,
Fellow of Trinity Coll., Cambridge. 9s. 6d.

Guide to the Hebrew Student. By
H. H. BERNARD. 10s. 6d.

The Psalms in Hebrew, with Critical,
Exegetical, and Philological Commentary.
By G. PHILLIPS, B.D., Tutor of Queen's
College, Cambridge. Two Volumes. 32s.

Elements of Syriac Grammar. By
G. PHILLIPS, B.D. Second Edition. 10s.

Practical Arabic Grammar. By
DUNCAN STEWART. Octavo. 16s.

Lightning Source UK Ltd.
Milton Keynes UK
UKHW022315181122
412457UK00005BA/73

9 781356 914296